Food Pets Die For
Shocking Facts About Pet Food

ANN N. MARTIN

Foreword by
Shawn Messonnier, D.V.M.

NewSage Press
TROUTDALE, OREGON

Third Edition
Food Pets Die For:
Shocking Facts About Pet Food

Copyright 2008© Ann N. Martin

Third Edition published 2008   ISBN 978-0939165-56-8
First Edition published 1997   ISBN 0-939165-31-7
Second Edition published 2003   ISBN 0-939165-46-5

NewSage Press
PO Box 607
Troutdale, OR 97060-0607
503-695-2211
www.newsagepress.com

Cover and Book Design Sherry Wachter
Printed in the United States.

Distributed by Publishers Group West

Note to the reader: This book is an informational guide. Consult a veterinarian or animal nutritionist if you have concerns about your animal companion's diet or health.

Library of Congress Cataloging-in-Publication Data

Martin, Ann N., 1944-
Food pets die for: shocking facts about pet food / by Ann N. Martin; foreword by Shawn Messonier.–3rd ed.
      p. cm.
Includes bibliographical references and index.
ISBN 0-939165-56-2 (alk. paper)
1. Pets—Feeding and feeds. 2. Pets—Health. 3. Pets—Feeding and feeds—Contamination—United States. 4. Pets—Feeding and feeds—Contamination—Canada. 5. Pet food industry—United States. 6. Pet food industry—Canada.
I. Title.

SF414.M37 2008
63.19'29–dc22

                                                                            2008023314

3 4 5 6 7 8 9

Dedicated to the memory of
Tracy Ann Smith, 1950-2006.

Tracy was a NewSage Press copy editor extraordinaire,
who worked diligently on the first and second editions
of this book. Her lifelong love for animals, and
her commitment to good books, are entwined in
these pages. We will always remember Tracy.

Acknowledgments

Many individuals helped along the way as I updated and added new information for the third edition. First and foremost I want to acknowledge my publisher and editor, Maureen R. Michelson, who spent untold hours questioning my information, checking facts, and editing the material to make a rough manuscript a readable book. My sincere thank you, Maureen, for all you have done over the years since first publishing my book in 1997.

A special thank you to NewSage Press designer, Sherry Wachter, who made this book attractive and visually inviting.

I am grateful to Shawn Messonnier, D.V.M., Michael Fox, D.V.M., Alfred Plechner, D.V.M., and Martin Zucker for their willingness to support my work with kind words and endorsements. You are all people I admire for your work and your writing. I am humbled. To the many veterinarians and specialists in various fields with whom I have corresponded, you have added immeasurable information, which has provided insight into the various topics covered. Please know that you have played a very important role.

Chuck, my partner, my friend, thank you from the bottom of my heart for being there. Jamie, my son, without your computer knowledge my manuscript would have been lost, numerous times.

Thank you to my sister, Mary, for her remarkable photographs of Kodi, my beautiful Newfoundland. Congratulations for your award-winning photo of Kodi as a baby.

To my extended family—Darlene, Tina, Audrey, Sheila and their families—you are all a very important part of my life. My friends, worldwide, who have provided so much information, please know that without your input many questions would have been left unanswered.

Last, but not least, I feel tremendous gratitude for my four-legged family, both past and present, who have been my taste testers for a variety of my home-cooked meals. My current animal companions—two-year-old Kodi and twenty-two-year-old Simon—continue to inspire me in my work. I love you all.

A Special Endorsement

Every veterinarian should provide copies of this book for their clients, and everyone with a companion dog or cat should not be without it. Good nutrition is a cornerstone for health and disease prevention. Ann Martin documents how this cornerstone has been removed by the commercial pet food industry. They recycle and profit from the by-products of the human food industry, including the diseased and condemned parts of cruelly raised, factory-farmed animals. This practice puts millions of dogs, cats, and other animals, as well as humans at risk.

Food Pets Die For is part of the ongoing revolution in agriculture and the food industry that calls on informed consumers to support a more humane, organic, sustainable, and healthful food production system.

I am honored to again endorse this book in its third edition because Ann Martin's investigative writing has helped set the record straight on a multi-billion-dollar pet food industry. With this information we can all act responsibly by making informed choices for the health and well-being of our beloved animal companions.

—Michael W. Fox
Veterinarian, Bioethicist, and Author

CONTENTS

Ann N. Martin presents information that is informative, eye-opening, and groundbreaking in exposing the truth behind what is contained in many commercially-produced pet foods. While the information contained in *Foods Pets Die For* may appear controversial and will likely be dismissed by some, it is well-researched information.

She points out the dangers that are often present in many brands of commercial pet food and encourages you to learn more about just what is contained in that bag or can before you feed it to your pet. In short, Ann Martin presents an answer that at times is not too pleasant to the all-important question I pose: *Do you really know what your pet ate last night?*

As a practicing holistic veterinarian, I am constantly amazed that diet is often the most neglected part of a pet's health care. It's not that most pet owners don't want to feed their pets properly, it's just that they think they are doing so simply because they have purchased one of the "recommended premium foods" advertised or promoted by the pet store clerk or even by their own veterinarians.

I used to believe that simply recommending a "premium" food was enough. Somehow my limited knowledge of nutrition qualified me to believe that following the advice of a pet food company and then making that food available to my clients ensured they would feed a healthy diet.

When I decided to change my focus of treating disease to "healing pets" and began incorporating a holistic approach at my practice, I realized that the only thing "premium" about the diets I had recommended was the price!

By learning all I could about pet nutrition and the pet food industry, I have changed my recommendation. Now I know better. As Ann Martin discusses in this book, the best diet is a homemade one, using the freshest, most wholesome ingredients. Next best is a diet from a company that truly uses wholesome protein, fat, and carbohydrate sources in the diet, without relying on toxic chemicals and preservatives. Either diet choice can be made even better with proper nutritional supplementation.

In my pre-veterinary studies I was an animal science major. One of my favorite classes was meat science, where my classmates and I were taught how to properly process meat for the consumer. I was quite impressed that literally nothing from the slaughtered animal carcass was ever wasted. What wasn't wholesome for human consumption was sold to the pet food industry.

At the time, I appreciated that there was no waste in the processing plant. Now that I have learned more about pet nutrition, I'm not quite so impressed. The waste that ends up in our pets' food would be better used as fertilizer. The same meats that humans eat should be used in preparing a processed food for pets. The reason many companies rely on slaughterhouse waste for raw pet food ingredients is cost—it is simply cheaper to use the trash from the slaughterhouse than whole fresh meats and organs. No thought is given to what feeding waste products might do to a pet's health.

As a practicing veterinarian, I can honestly say that most of my clients would gladly spend a few extra dollars for their pets' food if it was made with quality ingredients and contributed to (rather than detracted from) their pets' health. No longer can we make cost an issue. As Ann Martin clearly explains, "If it had not been for the illness of my two dogs in 1990 I would likely still be feeding commercial pet foods, thinking I was doing what is best for my beloved pets. I would also still be paying vet bills almost on a monthly basis."

Yes, it's true: taking a holistic approach to pet care does usually save the pet owner money on veterinary bills. Starting with a wholesome diet is the first concern that should be addressed in any holistic pet care program.

If more people knew what is contained in many processed foods and complained to the manufacturers, I believe we would see more wholesome diets produced.

Use the information in this informative book and learn to feed your pet the best food possible. Good luck on your road to better pet health!

—SHAWN MESSONNIER, D.V.M.
The Natural Vet's Guide to
Preventing and Treating Cancer in Dogs

About the Photos in This Book

Many of the photographs in this book are portraits of cats and dogs who were waiting for a loving home while staying at the Marin Humane Society in Novato, California. For years, professional photographer Sumner Fowler has used his talents to bring the plight of homeless, abandoned, rescued, and relinquished cats and dogs to the attention of the public. His portraits capture the unique and individual character of each cat and dog longing for a second chance. Over the years, NewSage Press has used Sumner's photos on many of its book covers. May their beautiful faces inspire readers to consider their local humane society or shelter as a place to find their next animal companion.

We have also included photographs of some of Ann Martin's animal-companions, and her editor/publisher, Maureen Michelson's, animal companions. These loving cats and dogs have inspired them for years to write and publish books on pet nutrition in hopes that pet owners will learn to feed their animals healthy foods for long and happy lives. Everyone who has participated in the writing, production, and publication of this book—from writer to editor to designer—knows the love, loyalty, and companionship of a cat and/or dog.

Introduction to the Third Edition of
FOOD PETS DIE FOR

Since the publication of the first edition of *Food Pets Die For* in 1997, my research and investigation into the pet food industry has turned into an ongoing life pursuit. At the time, few pet owners had any idea how the pet food industry worked or what was actually in the pretty cans and bags of food they fed their animal companions.

This new edition of my book is the result of my investigation into the pet food industry since 1990. Slowly, a growing number of consumers began to question the unregulated, multi-billion-dollar pet food industry. In 1988, "Project Censored," sponsored by Sonoma State University's journalism department, chose my investigative writing on the pet food industry as one of the most socially significant news stories that had been overlooked, under-reported, or self-censored.

The second edition of *Food Pets Die For* was published in 2003, and its popularity as one the definitive exposés on the pet food industry made this book a grassroots bestseller. While many in the mainstream media dismissed my findings, pet owners began to spread the word that commercial pet food posed potential health problems.

Now, with the publication of the third edition, you will see that I still have many concerns about the pet food industry, its business practices, and the inferior pet foods they produce. With rare exception, most commercial foods are far from being balanced and nutritious.

In 2007, the largest recall in the history of the pet food industry shocked the public as manufacturers recalled more than 60 million bags and cans of pet food. In the end, an untold number of cats and dogs—perhaps thousands— died after eating food tainted with questionable products from China. This massive recall became a major wake-up call for millions of consumers, who in the past never even questioned what they fed their pets. This recall has led to more questioning of the industry, including a U.S. Senate hearing. Still, a year later, there are unanswered questions, pending lawsuits against pet food manufacturers, and ongoing concerns about commercial foods.

Every day since the 2007 recall, pet owners have contacted me, questioning what pet food is safe to feed their pets. Many do not have time to cook for their pets and they are looking for healthy alternatives. In this new edition, I list pet food companies that I consider reliable in their practices, and producing quality pet food with human-grade ingredients. This list is not definitive, but it is a solid beginning. I am continually looking at other pet food companies producing quality foods, and welcome suggestions.

Before recommending a particular pet food, I find out who actually makes the products that go into a company's food and where the ingredients originated. I ask manufacturers numerous questions, such as: "Do you make your own food in your own facility?" If not, "Is your food made by a co-packer?" If so, "Which co-packer?" "What inspections do you carry out on the ingredients, meat, grains, fats, oils, vitamins, minerals and amino acids used in the food?"

I also research to find out if the pet food company has been in a previous recall, and if so, what was the reason? I even ask if the pet food manufacturers participate in animal experimentation in any way. Sadly, there are major corporate pet food companies that spend millions every year on experiments that injure and kill animals.

If a reputable pet food company refuses to answer any of my questions, but I still think the company produces quality food, I note my concerns. I also warn readers to be vigilant in checking out pet foods, and I offer ways to do this. For starters, I explain how to read pet food labels, and what the listed ingredients might include—oftentimes an unsavory toxic mix.

Most importantly, I continue to make my case for cooking for animal companions as the best choice. I have included an assortment of easy, nutritious recipes and simple guidelines to begin making home-cooked meals for your pets. This does not have to be complicated or intimidating. In fact, it can be fun, and certainly an expression of love your animal companions will greatly appreciate.

Since 1990 I have fed my dogs and cats a homemade diet. The pet food industry and some veterinarians warn against home cooking, claiming pets are not receiving a "balanced diet." I completely disagree with this assessment. In fact, my experience over the years proves a homemade diet can extend the life of an animal companion and cut down on veterinary bills.

My pets, along with thousands of others who eat home-cooked meals, are outliving standard life spans for cats and dogs by years. For example, the lifespan of a giant-breed Newfoundland is approximately eight years. My Newfoundland, Charlie, was fourteen years old when he died. My cats have also lived long lives, well into their twenties, and died of old age. My cat, Yakkie, lived until he was twenty-seven.

Imagine if your animal companion regularly ate healthy, human-grade food. If you eat this way, and experience the benefits of good health, so will your dog or cat. *Bon appétit!*

—ANN N. MARTIN
April 2008

Food Pets Die For

Ann Martin's newest member
to the family, Kodi.

PHOTO: MARY CHAMBERS

I

The Truth About Commercial Pet Foods

The information in this book may not be easy to accept, but if you care about your animal companions, then keep reading. Since first writing the original edition of *Food Pets Die For* in 1997 and exposing what goes into those attractive cans and bags of commercial pet food, far more consumers are realizing that many of the claims made by commercial pet food companies about their products being "balanced and nutritional" are false. This reality hit home for millions of pet owners in March 2007 when the largest pet food recall in history began to unfold. There are still many unanswered questions about this recall that involved more than one hundred pet food companies and millions of bags and cans of their products.

I first began to question the pet food industry in 1990 after my two dogs, Louie, a Saint Bernard, and Charlie, a Newfoundland, got severely ill after eating dry dog food. This compelled me to investigate commercial pet food ingredients and the pet food manufacturers. Quickly, I learned that this is a multi-billion dollar industry that in many ways is self-regulated.

I also learned that there are many deplorable ingredients that legally can be used in pet foods as sources of protein—in particular, euthanized cats and dogs, diseased cattle and horses, road kill, dead zoo animals, and meat not fit for human consumption. In addition, fiber sources in many foods are composed of the leftovers from the food chain, including beet pulp, the residue of sugar beets, peanut hulls, and even sawdust sweepings from the floor of the rendering plant!

1

Some people will question if it is really possible that so many disgusting ingredients can be legally added to commercial pet food. I have taken great care to responsibly make my case about the dangers of most commercial pet foods and to document the sources.

Since the massive pet food recall in March 2007, consumers have learned that many of the ingredients used in pet food as well as human food, are being sourced from China. Contaminated rice protein and wheat gluten from China caused illness and death in hundreds, maybe thousands of cats and dogs. Imported foods from countries such as China, with questionable food safety regulations, have made millions of consumers wary about both pet food and human food.

The percentage of imported foods subject to regulatory inspections has steadily dropped in recent years, however, the proportion of imported food used in domestic manufacturing in the United States has skyrocketed. Don Lee, a reporter for the *Los Angeles Times*, wrote, "China exported $2.5 billion of food ingredients to the United States and the rest of the world in 2006, an increase of 150% from just two years earlier."[1]

Less than one percent of all human food imported from China is checked before its entry into the United States. I believe it is only a matter of time before consumers see more major recalls—for pet food and human food. We need reliable regulations on all imported foods, including any ingredients added to pet foods.

Research

The information in the third edition of *Food Pets Die For* reflects years of persistent questioning and research into the pet food industry. I have gone back to government agencies, pet food industry representatives, rendering industry representatives, independent organizations, pet food companies, and individuals and veterinarians with many questions, numerous times.

Over the past eighteen years of researching the pet food industry, there have been times when I was horrified with what I learned. There are other times when I was extremely frustrated with the run-around I received from government agencies, organizations involved with the pet food industry, the rendering industry, and at times, veterinary research centers. What has kept me going is the hope that pet owners will read my findings and be convinced that their pets' health is directly related to what they eat—and that most commercial pet foods are garbage.

Many years ago I learned that if I wanted to get any reliable information from various United States and Canadian governments I did not write to them with my questions and simply expect them to give me honest answers. For several years, I dealt with bureaucratic run-around and delay tactics from both countries' governments. I was constantly referred to someone else for an answer. This still goes on. Government agencies are notorious for beating around the bush, saying a lot yet saying nothing.

Now I file Freedom of Information (FOI) requests. Through trial and error I have learned how to be specific regarding the information I request under the FOI. Over the years government agencies have sent documents that have been remotely close to what I had requested, but not what I asked for. So, I had to go back again with a more specific request. This was the case when requesting the results for tests the Food and Drug Administration (FDA) undertook on dry commercial pet food that contained pentobarbital. (See Chapter Five.) It took nearly three years to obtain that information and I received it only after I got help from a lawyer.

I have learned that the multi-billion dollar pet food industry wants to continue using the same dubious ingredients it has used for years, and increase bottom-line profits. Until consumers demand change, and government pressure insists on better regulation, change will only come in small increments. Getting answers may take time. Getting changes, and perhaps regulations, will take even more time—but it is something that anyone who cares about their pets must demand.

If it had not been for the illness of my two dogs in 1990, I probably would have kept feeding my animal companions commercial pet foods, thinking I was doing what was best for my beloved pets. I would also have paid veterinary bills almost on a monthly basis. And ultimately, I would not have been aware that after my animal companions died, there was a good possibility their remains may have ended up at a rendering plant.

Pet Carcasses in the Human Food Chain?

While researching the latest information on the 2007 pet food recall, I came across disturbing information that indicates rendered cat and dog carcasses could be entering the human food chain. Evidence leads to the strong possibility that shrimp, fish and eel grown on fish farms in China and other Asian countries, could be eating "tankage" shipped from renderers in California.

Dry rendered tankage is defined as material from rendering plants that is ground, heated to release the fat and drive off the moisture, percolated to drain off the free fat, and then pressed to remove yet more fat from the solids. This tankage could contain rendered cat and dog carcasses. This means that rendered dogs and cats, which are allowed to be a part of "tankage" in California rendering plants, could be destined for shrimp and fish food in China, Japan, Singapore, Taiwan, and South Korea.

California is the only state that classifies this material as tankage. It is perfectly legal for tankage to be shipped outside of California and be labeled as "meat and bone meal." I have contacted the USDA several times to verify whether or not this is true and have received no reply.

In March 2004, Bill Gorman, president of West Coast Rendering in California told Kate Berry, a reporter with the *Los Angeles Business Journal*, "We've been building a mountain [of euthanized cats and dogs] in the back of our place." He told the reporter he only had room "for another 600 tons of dog and cat byproduct in silos behind the Vernon plant."[2] These euthanized animals had been stockpiled because numerous Asian countries had banned imports of beef by-products due to the mad cow scare in the United States in December 2003. The ban was lifted in the summer of 2004, and shipping tankage to Asia resumed.

Leo Grillo is the founder of D.E.L.T.A. Rescue based in Acton, California, which claims to be the largest no-kill, care-for-life animal shelter worldwide. Grillo wrote about his investigators who followed trucks carrying "protein meal" made from rendered companion animals at the West Coast Rendering facility to the ports where they were loaded for shipment to Pacific Rim countries. Grillo explained that this material is fed to the "farmed fish and seafood that comes back to the United States and is sold in our supermarkets."[3] China is the leading exporter of seafood to the United States.

An article in the *World Daily News* reported that China is raising "most of its fish products in water contaminated with raw sewage and compensating by using dangerous drugs and chemicals, many of which are banned by the Food and Drug Administration [FDA]."[4] The article goes on to say that the FDA inspection process of China's seafood has worsened over the years "from 0.88 percent in 2003 to 0.59 percent in 2006—this while seafood consumption in the U.S. was rising and more of that seafood was coming from China."

In the ever-broadening mystery and madness surrounding global food imports and exports, for both human foods and pet foods, it is becoming incredibly difficult to track the true source(s) of food for ourselves and for our animal companions. The case for buying locally, and supporting sustainability within one's own community, grows stronger by the day as we face expanding food problems—for both humans and pets. In the meantime, I plan to avoid fish and seafood from Asian fish farms.

Making an Informed Choice

In order to understand the problems with the commercial pet food industry it is first helpful to understand what can legally go into pet foods, how the product is made, and how multi-billion dollar commercial pet food companies work. Several chapters will explain all of this. Then, once you have the facts, you can decide the next best step for you and feeding your animal companions. The latter part of this book offers information on diet considerations for your dog and/or cat, along with easy recipes.

My hope is that the information in my books will help pet owners make informed choices about what they feed their pets. If people feed their animal companions healthy diets, and in turn, pay closer attention to their own diets, both humans and animal companions will live longer happier lives.

Felicity waits at a humane society for a family
to love.
PHOTO: SUMNER FOWLER

2

Unravelling the Mystery Ingredients in Commercial Pet Food

*I*n recent years, some small pet food companies have begun to make healthy pet food using only human grade ingredients. When you read the labels on these wholesome pet foods, most likely you will recognize all of the ingredients listed, such as chicken, zucchini, squash, celery, and turkey. With these natural pet foods, what you see is what you get.

The standard fare from most commercial pet food companies is a mystery, and the long list of ingredients indecipherable. Despite highly touted claims of being balanced and nutritious, most commercial pet food products are anything but that. In fact, many of the ingredients are potentially harmful and composed of the dregs from slaughterhouses and the rendering business.

Even some of the "premium foods" promoted by pet food companies are really not any different from their standard line—other than being more expensive. As explained in Chapter Eight, *Pet Food Recalls*, many pet food companies get their lines of wet or dry food from one or two manufacturers that produce hundreds of pet food brands under various private-label names. These lines of food can range from the cheapest supermarket brands right up to the high priced "premium" foods, yet it may basically all be the same inferior product from the same pet food manufacturer. The bags and cans may have different attractive designs with claims of being "completely nutritious" and "balanced," but in my opinion, this is simply false advertising.

So, how do you determine if a particular pet food is nutritious or not? Ultimately, the best defense is to feed your animal companions human-grade food, either home-cooked, or made by pet food companies that only use human-grade foods. (In later chapters, I offer many options for cooking meals or for buying natural pet foods.) If you decide to feed your animal companions commercial pet foods that do not use human-grade ingredients, be sure to read the labels. Some foods are worse than others. And even then, *buyer beware.*

Deciphering Pet Food Labels

Pet food labels can be deceiving—they only provide half the story. The other half of the story is hidden behind obscure ingredients listed on the label, or they are not listed at all because they were added *before* the product reached the pet food company. Even conscientious consumers cannot possibly detect the hidden ingredients that can be legally put in pet food. Only about half the actual contents of the pet food are listed on the label due to minimal legal regulations in the pet food industry.

In addition, it is not easy to understand what the list of ingredients truly implies. The only way that I have figured this out is by unearthing the information slowly, bit by bit. I have been chipping away at these mystery-labeling practices since 1992. For instance, it took me awhile to figure out what certain words on a pet food label actually mean. A good example is the ingredient "meat by-product." The word "meat" sounds good and implies protein, but "meat by-product" can include a variety of unsavory animal parts. According to the Association of American Feed Control Officials (AAFCO), "Meat by-product is the nonrendered, clean parts of slaughtered mammals other than the meat."

Under AAFCO guidelines, acceptable meat by-product can include animal lungs, spleens, kidneys, brains, livers, blood, bones, low-temperature fatty tissue, and stomachs and intestines freed of their contents. The guidelines indicate that "meat by-product" can even include livers infested with worms (liver flukes) or diseased with cirrhosis. Lungs can be filled with pneumonia. If an animal is diseased and declared unfit for human consumption, the carcass is acceptable for pet food. Even parts of animals, such as "stick marks,"—the area of the body where animals have been injected with antibiotics, hormones, or other drugs—are cut from the carcasses intended for human consumption and used for meat by-product in pet food.

Dead Dogs and Cats as a Protein Source

The most objectionable source of protein for pet food is euthanized cats and dogs. (See Chapter Four.) It is a common practice for thousands of euthanized dogs and cats to be delivered to rendering plants, daily, and thrown into rendering vats—along with pet collars, I.D. tags, and plastic bags—to become part of an ingredient called "meat meal." If you see the term "meat meal" listed as an ingredient, there is no guarantee that the pet food does not contain euthanized cats and dogs.

Note the difference between the terms "meat meal" and "meat by-products," which are commonly listed as ingredients on pet food labels. The term "meat meal" refers to material from rendering plants that is sent to pet food manufacturers. The term "meat by-products" refers to the material sent to pet food companies directly from the slaughterhouse and does not involve rendering.

I have listed some of the ingredients frequently included on pet food labels. These definitions are from AAFCO's "Ingredient Definitions." Note that when you read descriptions that include "clean flesh" or "clean parts," this means that the material is basically devoid of any extraneous matter such as hair, fur, and stomach contents. However, the idea of creating "clean parts" in the rendering process seems misleading at best, and in my opinion, a complete misnomer. In an article written by David C. Cooke, "Animal Disposal: Fact and Fiction," Cooke noted, "Can you imagine trying to remove the fur and stomach contents from 600,000 tons of dogs and cats prior to cooking them? It would seem that either the Association of American Feed Control Officials' [AAFCO] definition of meat meal or meat and bone meal should be redefined or it needs to include a better description of good factory practices."[1]

Meat, Poultry, and Fish Sources

My research shows that the meat used in pet food is sourced in the United States, and arrives at the pet food manufacturer as a "meat meal" or "meat and bone meal." Lamb is the only imported meat source, coming from Australia and New Zealand.

The following are definitions provided by the AAFCO for explaining ingredients acceptable under certain terms for labeling.

Meat: AAFCO defines "meat" as the clean flesh derived from slaughtered mammals. This mammal flesh is limited to the part of the striate muscle that is skeletal or what is found in the tongue, diaphragm, heart, or esophagus. AAFCO stipulates that the flesh is "with or without the accompanying and overlying fat and the portions of the skin, sinew, nerve, and blood vessels that normally accompany the flesh."

When you read on a pet food label that the product contains "meat," you are getting blood vessels, sinew, and so on. Meat is not rendered but comes directly from slaughterhouses. Again, this is called "meat by-product" and can contain many unsavory and/or diseased animal parts.

Meat meal: AAFCO defines "meat meal" as the rendered product from mammal tissue exclusive of blood, hair, hoof, hide, trimmings, manure, stomach, and rumen contents, except in such amounts as may occur unavoidably in good processing practices. (The rumen is the first stomach, also called the cud, of a cud-chewing animal.)

Poultry-by-product meal: This consists of ground, rendered, clean parts of slaughtered poultry, including necks, feet, undeveloped eggs, and intestines, exclusive of feathers, except in such amounts as might occur unavoidably in good processing practices.

Poultry-hatchery by-product: This ingredient can include a mixture of eggshells, infertile and unhatched eggs, and culled chicks that have been cooked, dried, and ground with or without removal of part of the fat.

Poultry by-product: This can include non-rendered clean parts of slaughtered poultry such as heads, feet, and viscera, free of fecal content and foreign matter except in such trace amounts as might occur unavoidably in good factory practice.

Hydrolyzed poultry feather: AAFCO considers this another source of protein—not digestible protein, but protein nonetheless. This product results from a pressure treatment of clean, intact feathers from slaughtered poultry, free of additives, and/or accelerators. (An accelerator makes the feathers compost faster.)

Fish: If you live with a cat, just open a can of food that contains fish and watch kitty come running. The parts used in pet foods are fish heads, tails, fins, bones, and viscera. If the label lists "fish," this means that the fish parts come directly from the fish processing plants and do not go through the rendering process.

R.L. Wysong, D.V.M., states that because the entire fish is not used for most commercial pet foods, it does not contain many of the fat-soluble vitamins, minerals, and omega-3 fatty acids necessary for good nutrition. When the entire fish is used for commercial pet food, oftentimes it is because the fish contains a high level of mercury or other toxin making it unfit for human consumption. Tuna is used in many cat foods because of its strong odor, which many cats find irresistible. However, as I discuss in Chapter Nine, "Cooking for Cats," fish as a regular protein source can cause health problems in most cats.

Fishmeal: rendering residue from the fish processing plants creates this product. "Fish meal" might include heads, tails, innards, and blood. It is generally higher in protein quality than meat meal and bone meal. The AAFCO defines fishmeal as "clean, dried, ground tissue of undecomposed whole fish or fish cuttings, either or both, with or without the extraction of part of the oil." It appears that the vast percentage of fishmeal is from the fish industries in the United States, as far as I can discern.

Unsavory Protein Sources Allowed in Pet Food

According to AAFCO, there are a number of other sources that can make up the protein in pet foods. NOTE OF CAUTION: If you have a weak stomach, proceed at your own risk.

Hydrolyzed hair is made from clean hair treated by heat and pressure to produce a product suitable for animal feeding. This includes the hair from cattle, horses, pigs, or other animals who have been slaughtered.

Spray-dried animal blood is produced from clean, fresh animal blood, exclusive of all extraneous material such as hair, stomach belching (contents of stomach), and urine, except in such traces as might occur unavoidably in good factory practices. Blood from these animals can be used in pet food, either mixed with other materials in the rendering process, or formed into the meat chunks that are found in some canned foods.

Dehydrated food-waste is any and all animal and vegetable produce picked up from basic food processing sources or institutions, including garbage from hospitals, restaurants, and grocery stores. The produce has to be picked up daily or sufficiently often so that no decomposition is evident. With this ingredient, it seems that what you don't see won't hurt you.

Dehydrated garbage is composed of artificially dried animal and vegetable waste collected frequently so that harmful decomposition has not set in. AAFCO guidelines stipulate that dehydrated garbage should be separated from crockery, glass, metal, string, and similar materials. This might include waste from butcher shops or manufacturing plants that process fruits and vegetables.

Dehydrated paunch products (ingested food and water) are composed of the contents of the rumen of slaughtered cattle, dehydrated at temperatures over 212° F. (100° C.) to a moisture content of 12 percent or less. Such dehydration is designed to destroy any pathogenic bacteria.

Dried poultry waste is an animal waste product composed primarily of processed excreta that has been artificially dehydrated to a moisture content not in excess of 15 percent. According to AAFCO, "It shall contain not less than 12 percent crude protein, not more than 40 percent crude fiber, including straw, wood shavings, and so on, and not more than 30 percent ash." This material is often obtained from factory farming operations.

Dried swine waste is an animal waste product composed primarily of swine excreta that has been artificially dehydrated to a moisture content not in excess of 15 percent. AAFCO guidelines state, "It shall contain not less than 20 percent crude protein, not more than 35 percent crude fiber, including other material such as straw, wood shavings, or acceptable bedding materials, and not more than 20 percent ash." This often comes from large hog operations.

Undried, processed animal waste product is composed of excreta, with or without the litter (litter is the ground covering in the chicken pens) from poultry, ruminants, or any other animal except humans. This may or may not include other feed ingredients. AAFCO stipulates that this product "shall contain no more than 30 percent combined wood, wood shavings, litter, dirt, sand, rocks, and similar extraneous materials."

Grain Sources

In addition to listing protein sources that can be used in pet foods, AAFCO also has an extensive list of various grains that can be used in pet foods, horse feed, and cattle feed.

Corn: **This** is the main ingredient in dry food for dogs and cats. According to AAFCO, there is a long list of corn products that can be used in pet food. These include, but are not limited to, the following ingredients.

Corn flour: This is the fine-size, hard flinty portion of ground corn containing little or none of the bran or germ.

Corn bran: This is the outer coating of the corn kernel with little or none of the starchy part of the germ.

Corn gluten meal: This is the dried residue from corn after the removal of the larger part of the starch and germ, and the separation of the bran by the process employed in the wet milling manufacture of cornstarch or syrup, or by enzymatic treatment of the endosperm.

Note: Many dry cat foods contain corn in one form or another as the prime ingredient. In one dry cat food I found corn in four different forms. This is not good for cats who require at least half of their diet to be a protein source. Also, grains do not supply a cat with sufficient amounts of arachidonic acid (an essential fatty acid), vitamin A, or vitamin B-12. In addition, cats require a meat source to obtain the amino acid, taurine. Most dry commercial cat foods lack the natural form of taurine, so it is added as a supplement to the grains.

Wheat: Many pet foods include wheat, and AAFCO guidelines give several terms for wheat products.

Wheat flour: This consists principally of wheat flour together with fine particles of wheat bran, wheat germ, and the offal from the "tail of the mill." The term "tail of the mill" simply means the floor sweepings of leftovers in the mill after everything has been processed from the wheat.

Wheat middlings and shorts: These are also categorized as the fine particles of wheat germ, bran, flour, and offal from the tail of the mill. Basically these ingredients amount to nothing more than the sweepings from the mill floor.

Wheat germ meal: This consists chiefly of wheat germ together with some bran and middlings or shorts.

The Deceptive Practice of "Splitting" in Labeling

Corn and wheat are usually the first ingredients listed on both dry dog and cat food labels. However, some pet food companies list the product ingredients in such a way that the number one ingredient listed is a protein product. For example, in one well-known dry cat food the ingredients on the label are listed in this order:

> poultry by-product meal, ground yellow corn, wheat,
> corn gluten meal, soybean meal, brewers rice, etc.

Most people reading this label might assume that the "poultry by-product meal" is the prime ingredient providing an ample source of protein. Wrong. In fact, corn is the prime ingredient for this cat food. To make it appear that the protein source is the number one ingredient in the pet food, the company split the corn into two categories; ground yellow corn and corn gluten meal. But if you add the *total* amount of all forms of corn used, versus the protein source, there is far more corn.

In the pet food industry, this labeling practice is called "splitting." If corn is listed in more than one form, then it might be the prime ingredient in the food instead of the poultry meal and would have to be listed first on the label. Pet food companies want you to think their product contains mostly protein, so they "split" the corn products. This can be problematic for consumers who believe a dry food is sufficient for their animal companions, especially cats. Cats are carnivores and require a good source of meat in their diets. So pet owners who think it's okay to just feed their cats a dry food are not providing a healthy diet.

Toxic Substances in Grain

The contamination of grains used in pet food, particularly mycotoxins, can be deadly. Mycotoxins are toxic substances produced by fungi in moldy grains and they are found in rye, corn, barley, oats, wheat, peanuts, Brazil nuts, pecans, and walnuts. More than three hundred types of mycotoxins exist worldwide.

The most common mycotoxins are aflatoxins B1. These are known carcinogens in laboratory animals and presumably in our pets. Fumonisin B1 and B2 are molds that are common natural contaminants of corn. Animal studies have indicated that the B1 variety of this toxin is carcinogenic.

Ochratoxin A, found mainly in cereal grains, corn, barley, wheat, and oats, is another carcinogen. Ochratoxin A is not completely destroyed in food processing and cooking.

Deoxynivalenol (DON,) also known as vomitoxin, is a common contaminate of wheat, barley, rye, and corn. Pets who eat grains contaminated with vomitoxin can have symptoms that include vomiting, diarrhea, and refusing to eat.

In addition, many of the grains used in commercial pet foods contain levels of carcinogenic herbicides, pesticides, and fungicides. These are grains that did not pass inspection for use in human foods because of the levels of carcinogens and mycotoxins: however, they are deemed fit for use in pet foods. Little, if any, testing or research is undertaken to determine levels of these toxic substances in pet foods.

Additional Low-Grade Pet Food Ingredients

In addition to the main sources of ingredients used in commercial pet foods there are other ingredients that can be added, according to AAFCO. These ingredients may offer little or no nutritional value, but bulk up the pet food content.

Beet pulp: The dried residue from sugar beet is added for fiber, but it is primarily sugar.

Soybean meal: This is obtained by grinding the flakes that remain after using a solvent extract to remove most of the oil from soybeans.

Powdered cellulose: This ingredient is purified, mechanically disintegrated cellulose. It is a white, odorless, tasteless product prepared by processing alpha cellulose obtained as a pulp from fibrous plant material. The primary cell wall of green plants is made of cellulose. Powdered cellulose is used as a bulking agent in pet foods.

Sugar foods by-products: This ingredient is created by grinding and mixing inedible portions derived from the preparation and packaging of sugar-based food products such as candy, dry-packaged drinks, dried gelatin mixes, and similar food products that are largely composed of sugar. Sugar provides calories and makes foods more palatable.

Ground almond and peanut shells: These shells are finely ground and considered another source of fiber. Digestion would probably not be a problem, but the nutritional value is questionable.

Fats in Pet Food

Fats can be sprayed directly on pet food or mixed with the other ingredients. Fats give off a pungent odor that entices your pet to eat the food, even if it is garbage. These fats are often sourced from restaurant grease, which is likely to be rancid and certainly unfit for human consumption. Another main source of fat comes from the rendering plant. It is directly extracted from the tissues of mammals and/or poultry in the commercial rendering process described in the next section.

The Rendering Process

Before I began learning about what goes into commercial pet foods, I knew nothing about rendering plants or how product for pet food was manufactured. To say the least, this has been eye-opening. Rendering facilities have been around for hundreds of years, yet the general public knows very little about this industry. And I am sure that most people do not know that a lot of the by-product created by rendering plants ends up in commercial pet food.

Renderers accept the waste and leftovers from our modern society. This includes animals picked up by dead stock removal companies; dead zoo animals; road kill too large to be buried at the side of the road; restaurant and grocery store garbage, including the Styrofoam trays and plastic wrap; and hundreds of thousands of euthanized cats and dogs. (See Chapter Four for more information.)

Slaughterhouses also provide renderers with the leftovers from slaughtered animals not fit for human consumption. Before slaughterhouses ship these animal parts and by-product used for pet food to the rendering plant, the by-product is "denatured." This means slaughterhouse workers spray crude carbolic acid, cresylic disinfectant, or citronella on the dregs of the slaughterhouse that will become pet food product.

Keep in mind that all of these "denaturing products" are toxic. Cresylic acid is a tar-oil derivative that has replaced fuel oil as a denaturing substance.

In the United States, the Occupational Safety and Health Administration (OSHA) classifies both crude carbolic acid and cresylic as "poison."

For example, when a whole beef or swine carcass has been condemned, the denaturing product is injected into the entire carcass. If meat inspectors condemn only parts of an animal, the United States Department of Agriculture (USDA) requires that "before an approved denaturing agent is applied, the product must be freely slashed so that pieces are less than 4" in diameter. This allows the denaturant to contact all parts of the product."[6]

In Canada, the denaturing agent is Birkolene B. When I asked the Ministry of Agriculture what was in Birkolene B, the representative would not divulge its composition, stating its ingredients are a "trade secret." As of September 2007, Birkolene B is still the denaturing agent being used in Canada and the composition is still a deep dark secret.

At the rendering plant a machine slowly grinds the entire mess in huge vats. Then this product is cooked at temperatures between 220° F. and 270° F. (104.4° C. to 132.2° C.) for twenty minutes to one hour. The mixture is centrifuged (spun at a high speed) and the grease (or tallow) rises to the top and it is removed from the mixture. The grease becomes the source of animal fat in most pet foods. Oftentimes, when you open a standard can of dog food, you will see a top layer of fat. The centrifuged product is the source of that fat, which is meant to entice a hungry dog or cat.

After the renderers remove the grease, they dry the remaining material. Meat meal, and meat and bone meal are the end product of this rendering process. This dried material is usually found in dry pet food.

Can This Really Be True?

After reading the list of ingredients from AAFCO for the first time and not really believing that such ingredients could be used in pet food, I sent a fax to the chair of AAFCO. I asked, "Would the 'Feed Ingredient Definitions' apply to pet food as well as livestock feed?" The reply was as follows: "The feed ingredient definitions approved by AAFCO apply to all animal feeds, including pet foods, unless specific animal species restrictions are noted."[7] AAFCO confirmed what I hoped was not true. As of 2007, this is still the case: The ingredient definitions apply to both livestock and pet food.

I also found it difficult to believe that rendering plants produced much of the by-product used by commercial pet food companies. My disbelief has resulted in years of questioning government organizations, pet food manufacturers, renderers, animal-welfare organizations, and veterinarians.

The pet food industry claims to care about the health and welfare of our pets by providing complete and balanced diets. It is apparent from the ingredients used in these foods, and the lack of inspection of ingredients, that most pet food is nutritionally inferior or simply devoid of healthy and wholesome ingredients. We cannot expect our animal companions to enjoy good health and a long life if we feed them a diet that includes ingredients such as those mentioned in this chapter.

3
Questionable Vitamins, Minerals and Additives

On the labels of dog and cat food you will notice an extensive list of substances, many of which are odd names for added vitamins, minerals, and additives. In this chapter, I have listed some of the vitamins and minerals added to pet foods, along with simple healthy suggestions for natural and nutritious sources of these same vitamins and minerals for your pet's health. I also list some of the potentially harmful additives used to give pet food a long shelf life in the store.

NOTE OF CAUTION: When pet food manufacturers add vitamins, minerals, or additives to large vats of product being prepared for pet food, quantity control can be iffy. Many manufacturers add vitamin and mineral supplements in excess amounts called "overage" in order to compensate for vitamin destruction during the manufacturing process and over the shelf life of the product. This practice can be a gamble. In my case, my dogs got sick from a bag of dry food with excessive zinc. (I explain further in this chapter under "Minerals.")

In March 2007, Janet Grixti, a resident of Whitby, Ontario, Canada, filed a $50 million dollar, class action lawsuit against Royal Canin. The pet owner claims her chocolate lab, Mocha, suffered permanent kidney damage after ingesting foods produced by Royal Canin that contained excess levels of Vitamin D, which causes severe illness or death in pets.[1]

Vitamins in Pet Food

The following are vitamins commonly added to commercially manufactured pet foods.

Choline Chloride: member of the B complex. Natural sources include egg yolks, soy, cooked beef, chicken, and turkey livers.

Calcium Panthenate: vitamin B-5. Natural sources of B-5 include organ meats, eggs, fish, shellfish, lobsters, soybeans, and lentils.

Thiamin Mononitrate: vitamin B-1. Natural sources of B-1 include meats, poultry, whole grains nuts, legumes, and brewer's yeast.

Riboflavin Supplement: vitamin B-2. Natural sources of B-2 include milk, oysters, lean meat, leafy vegetables, mushrooms, and asparagus.

Pyridoxine Hydrochloride: vitamin B-6. Natural sources of B-6 include grains, bread, spinach, green beans, and cereals.

Folic Acid: vitamin B-9. Natural sources of Folic Acid or B-9 include liver, brewer's yeast, beets, turnips, asparagus, spinach, and dark leafy greens.

Ascorbic Acid: vitamin C. Natural sources of vitamin C include strawberries, citrus fruits, turnip greens, cabbage, sweet potatoes, broccoli, carrots, peas, squash, and parsley.

Vitamin D. Cholecalciferol, methionine, a source of D-3. Natural sources include sunlight, milk (fortified), cheese, whole eggs, liver and salmon.

Menadione Dimethylprimidinol Bisulfite: source of vitamin K. Leafy green vegetables such as kale, broccoli, spinach and collards are the best natural sources of vitamin K.

NOTE OF CAUTION: Regarding sources of vitamin K, there is a lot of controversy around menadione dimethylprimidinol bisulfite and its use in commercial pet foods as a source of vitamin K. This is a cheap source of Vitamin K that can be used in dry and canned foods as well as supplements and treats.

According to the Dog Food Project, an online forum with pet nutrition consultant, Sabine Contreras, "Menadione, also known as vitamin K-3, is a synthetic version of vitamin K."[2]

Technically, menadione is not even a vitamin, but a precursor that is converted in the body after ingestion. Vitamin K is fat soluble, while menadione derivatives are water-soluble and bypass the natural pathway of utilization by the body.

According to The Dogfood Project, menadione "causes cytotoxicity in liver cells, damages the natural vitamin K, causes allergic reactions and eczema, and causes irritation of skin and mucous membranes." Because of this questionable source of vitamin K, pet owners need to avoid foods that contain the synthetic form of vitamin K.

Minerals in Pet Food

The primary minerals added to pet food include zinc, iron, and copper. In some cases, these minerals can cause serious health problems for pets, particularly if you happen to get a bag of pet food that has an inordinate amount of minerals added. This was how my dogs initially got sick in 1990. After they had gotten sick repeatedly, vomiting on several occasions after eating the dry dog food, I had the food tested at an independent lab. The test results showed a zinc level *twenty times higher* than the daily recommended dose of 50 parts per million (ppm).

I contacted several veterinarians versed in toxicology who explained that zinc levels in excess of 1,000 ppm can be toxic for dogs. The Recommended Daily Allowance (RDA) for dogs is approximately 50 mg.. No wonder my dogs got seriously ill.

Other minerals often listed on a pet food label include:

Iron proteinate, ferrous carbonate, and ferrous sulfate: These minerals are necessary for the production of hemoglobin. Deficiencies will manifest themselves as anemia and fatigue. NOTE OF CAUTION: Ferrous sulfate can deplete vitamin E, which many "natural" pet foods use as a preservative. [3] Natural sources of iron include liver, kidney, lean meats, shellfish, fruits, nuts, whole grains, leafy vegetables, and blackstrap molasses.

Copper oxide and copper proteinate: These are necessary for converting the iron into hemoglobin. The liver stores the excess copper that the body is unable to use. Excess copper can result in liver disease. For example, Bedlington Terriers can inherit hemolytic anemia, characterized by an abnormal accumulation of copper in the liver.

Copper sulfate: This is a cheap copper supplement that the pet food industry chose to add to pet foods. It is in many pet foods, however, it may pose a major threat to your pet's health. Copper has been described in a toxicology research paper undertaken by four universities as "highly corrosive to plain steel, iron, and galvanized pipes."[4] People handling this material have been advised to wear boots, protective gloves, and goggles, yet this material may be added to both livestock and pet food.

Copper sulfate is stored in the liver, brain, heart, kidneys, and muscles of livestock who ingest it through the feed. Copper is stable in heat, cold, and light although there is slight decomposition at temperatures around 392° F. (200° C.) However, in the rendering process temperatures usually do not exceed 270° F. (132.2° C.), so it is highly likely that the copper sulfate in slaughtered cattle will be intact when rendered into pet food. This means that in addition to pet food companies adding the copper supplement, the mineral could also be present in meat by-product made from rendered cattle used in pet food.

Preservatives and Additives in Pet Foods

Preservatives are added to numerous ingredients that are later combined to make pet food. For instance, commercial pet food companies usually purchase large quantities of "pre-mixes"—vitamins and minerals already mixed together. These pre-mixes include preservatives. Other ingredients in pet foods with preservatives are meats and fats. By the end of the manufacturing process, pet food is loaded with preservatives from several different sources.

In addition, pet food manufacturers add artificial flavors, garlic, cheese, and bacon to make the food more palatable. The preservatives plus these added flavors are then doused with food dyes that turn the gray matter a bright red to give pet owners the impression that the dog or cat food is wholesome and fresh.

Some of the main preservatives to watch for when reading pet food labels include the following:

BHA (butylated hydroxyanisole), and **BHT** (butylated hydroxytoluene), two preservatives that have long been suspected of being carcinogenic. Both are chemical antioxidants that prevent the fatty contents of pet food from becoming rancid. Pet foods have an endless shelf life with these preservatives.

Wendell Belfield, D.V.M., has questioned the dubious ingredients in pet foods for years. Dr. Belfield shared with me a letter he wrote to the Center for Veterinary Medicine (CVM) in 2002 challenging the unnecessary use of these preservatives. He warned the CVM, "Chemicals such as BHA and BHT, which can initiate birth defects, and damage to liver and kidneys are commonly used preservatives."[5]

BHA and BHT preservatives are also found in the human food chain. BHA is used to keep fats from becoming rancid and can be found in butter, cereals, chewing gum, snack foods, baked goods, and meats. BHT prevents oxidative rancidity of fats and preserves food color, odor, and flavor. However, keep in mind that we are not ingesting these preservatives at every meal, whereas companion animals might be if they are eating the same processed pet food daily.

Ethoxyquin. This is another antioxidant preservative that has since been proven to be highly toxic to animals. I first wrote about this dangerous preservative in the early 1990s. Due to protests from many pet owners, ethoxyquin is not as prevalent as it once was. Yet, it is still approved by the FDA/CVM as an acceptable preservative in pet food.

Ethoxyquin was developed by The Monsanto Company, a multinational, agricultural biotechnology corporation. Monsanto developed ethoxyquin in the 1950s as a rubber stabilizer and later used this preservative as a pesticide and insecticide. By the 1980s, Monsanto had developed a refined version that has been used extensively in pet foods.

The nonprofit, animal advocacy organization, Animal Protection Institute (API), stated in a 1996 report: "Ethoxyquin has been associated with immune deficiency syndrome, leukemia, blindness, skin, stomach, spleen and liver cancer in companion animals."[6]

Many pet food companies state that they do not add this substance to their foods. However, what they neglect to mention is that the suppliers of the raw material used in pet foods—the meat and fats—can add ethoxyquin before they ship it to the pet food company. Unfortunately, if the pet food company does not know ethoxyquin was added, then they do not need to state this on the label. Pet food companies simply have to state what *they* have added, not what their suppliers have added to the raw material.

NOTE OF CAUTION: If you ever see ethoxyquin listed on a can or bag of pet food, *stay away from that product*. And if you don't see ethoxyquin listed as an ingredient, there is no guarantee that the preservative was not used somewhere along the way in the mysterious development of the pet food product.

China as a Supplier

China is the largest supplier of a variety of vitamins, minerals, and amino acids that are used in pet food. According to Steven Wirick, Chief Operating Officer of Solid Gold pet foods, they take extra care to use only the best ingredients. However, they have had trouble locating a source for taurine outside of China. "We have made an exhaustive search for a source of taurine manufactured in the United States, but unfortunately, there is none. To our knowledge, all taurine used in pet products and most human products is manufactured in China."[7] I want to note that Solid Gold is a high-quality pet food. (See Chapter Ten.)

Given the massive pet food recall of 2007 due to questionable products and practices from China's manufacturers, we need to be very cautious. At this point, I seriously question how safe the supplements are in commercial pet foods. There is no guarantee that contamination will not happen again.

4

Animal Carcasses
as a Protein Source

*A*s this third edition of *Food Pets Die For* goes to press, cats and dogs from shelters and veterinary clinics throughout the United States and Canada are still being rendered to make a protein source called "meat meal." Rendering plants then sell this meat meal to pet food manufacturers. It is still legal to render cat and dog carcasses, along with a variety of other animal remains listed below, to make a protein source for pet food.

Pet food manufacturers throughout the United States and Canada vehemently deny using "meat meal" that includes rendered cat and dog carcasses. *Renderer: The National Magazine of Rendering*, also denies that rendering plants mix pet carcasses for rendering along with the remains of slaughterhouses and other animal by-products. If these claims by pet food manufacturers and rendering plants are true, then I have to question *where* the millions of carcasses from euthanized cats and dogs are ending up?

I continue to delve into this question of rendered cat and dog carcasses and indeed, pet remains are still rendered for "meat meal" in pet food and possibly for "tankage" used to feed shrimp, eels, and a variety of farmed fish that are then bought and eaten by humans. (See Chapter One.)

When questioned about dog and cat carcasses as a source of protein in pet food, manufacturers vigorously deny that any of their products contain rendered companion animals. Technically, what lets many pet food manufacturers off the hook is that they do not directly know if pet carcasses are a part of the product they buy from a rendering plant. Pet food manufacturers also claim that they ask their suppliers not to include cats and dogs; however, I have yet to find a rendering plant that separates out dog and cat carcasses from other animal by-products to be rendered.

In addition, I have yet to find a pet food company that actually tests the raw material that it receives from a rendering plant to determine the sources of the protein. And as I explain later in this chapter, it is next to impossible to detect DNA from *any* species after it has been cooked in the rendering process, or after it has been manufactured into a finished pet food. Once you understand the rendering process, then it makes more sense *why* pet food companies can claim they have no knowledge of cat and dog carcasses rendered into a protein product.

The Rendering Process

Rendering plants are the last stop for society's leftovers, or what I call the dregs. Actually, renderers provide a necessary, though unpleasant, service. This is the end of the line for anything rejected for human consumption, and worse. A rendering plant takes unused animal by-products from a variety of sources: processing plants, supermarkets, butcher shops, restaurants, and any other source needing to dispose of animal by-products.

Renderers pick up "4-D" animals (dead, diseased, dying, and disabled) from fields or factory farms. Renderers also take diseased and condemned material from slaughterhouses; road kill, zoo animals, and euthanized dogs and cats from veterinary clinics and animal shelters. Add to that sordid mix thousands of pounds of recalled meat intended for human consumption, but rejected because of contamination. In the past, recalled meat could be sent to rendering plants to make pet food. However, in February 2008 the United States faced the biggest beef recall in its history—143 million pounds of beef. The USDA claimed this recalled beef would not end up in pet food, but exactly where it would all go had not been determined at the time this book went to press.

At the rendering plant, all of these carcasses, animal by-products, and unsavory leftovers are cut into chunks before being thrown into large vats for grinding and cooking. This results in the separation of the fat from what becomes the "meat meal." The fats rise to the top and are siphoned off to be used as the top layer in canned pet food. The fat may also be used in products for human use, such as cosmetics. The heavier material sinks to the bottom where it is dried to remove any additional fat. Then it is ground up. This is the "meat meal" that you find in many pet foods.

The National Renderers Association published a book on rendering that explains, in part, the process:

> The material is run through a grinder, which "reduces the raw material to a uniform particle size for material handling and improved heat transfer in the cooking (rendering) is generally accomplished with steam at temperatures of 240° to 290° F. (approximately 115° to 145° C.) for 40 to 90 minutes depending upon the type of system and materials. Most North American rendering systems are continuous-flow units."[1] Continuous flow cookers are horizontal steam-jacketed cylindrical vessels equipped with a mechanism that continuously moves the material horizontally through the cooker thus evaporating moisture and freeing fat from protein and bone. "The dehydrated slurry of fat and solids is discharged from the continuous cooker at a controlled rated. The next step separates liquid fat from solids. The solids go to a "screw press" that forms them into cakes, which are further processed into meal. The fat is pumped into tanks for transport.

Meat Meal Product

When I first began investigating the ingredients used in commercial pet food in the early 1990s, a veterinarian in the United States advised me that the use of pets in pet food was routine practice. Rendering is a cheap viable means of disposal for euthanized pets. If a euthanized pet is not cremated or taken home for burial, then the carcass most likely ends up in a rendering vat.

There are thousands of animal shelters throughout North America that euthanize millions of unwanted cats and dogs every year. Somehow, somewhere, these millions of carcasses must be disposed of. In a week's time, one busy veterinary clinic could have dozens of carcasses, and an overcrowded animal shelter could have hundreds of euthanized animals. Dead stock removal companies pick up the dead cats and dogs, and take them to rendering plants. The remains, along with collars, tags, and flea collars, are thrown in huge vats, along with other animal by-products.

In Los Angeles alone, more than 200 tons of dogs and cats are rendered each year. The statistics for the disposal of companion animals euthanized at shelters in 2002, as outlined by the National Animal Control Association (NACA) of the United States, show that annually 13 million household pets are euthanized. Of those, 30% are buried, 30% are cremated, and the remainder—about 5.2 million pet carcasses—are sent to rendering facilities.

I contacted John Mays at the NACA and asked for updated information on numbers of pets that are killed and the method of disposal. He replied, "Current stats regarding dead pet disposal are not currently offered."[2] He did not clarify *why* current stats are not offered—perhaps because of the controversy surrounding the rendering of cats and dogs?

—

Since the early 1990s, I have challenged commercial pet food companies' claims of innocence about the use of dog and cat carcasses in most pet foods. It is a well-established fact that rendering plants are oftentimes located near pet food companies. In my book, *Protect Your Pet,* I explain how rendering plants regularly pick up dead animals from veterinary clinics and shelters, and render them as a protein source.

Numerous times I have questioned the Pet Food Institute (PFI), the non-governmental organization that is the mouthpiece for major pet food manufacturers. The PFI asserts that it oversees the pet food industry in the United States—a business relationship I find as reassuring as a fox protecting the hen house! I have asked the PFI if the pet food manufacturers it represents test the raw material from rendering plants. In spring 2004, the PFI said that pet food companies do not test the raw material for the sources of animals rendered. Prior to the publication of the third edition of this book, I again went back to the PFI and asked if any of the pet food companies had changed their position and were now testing the raw material. The PFI chose not to respond.

Euthanized Pets and Rendering

Basically, there are two types of rendering plants: Plants that operate in conjunction with animal slaughterhouses or poultry processing plants are called "integrated rendering plants;" rendering plants that collect their raw materials from a variety of off site sources are called "independent rendering plants." Independent plants obtain animal by-product materials, including grease, blood, feathers, offal, and entire animal carcasses, from the following sources; butcher shops, supermarkets, restaurants, fast-food chains, poultry processors, slaughterhouses, farms, ranches, feedlots, and animal shelters."[3] All of the large rendering plants, including Darling International, Sacramento Rendering, West Coast Rendering, Baker Commodities Inc., Modesto Tallow, Carolina By-Products, Griffin Industries Inc., Rothsay, and Valley Proteins, are independent rendering plants.

Doug Anderson, president of Darling International, a large rendering company in Dallas, Texas, maintains that pet food companies try not to buy meat and bone meal from renderers that grind up cat and dog carcasses. "We do not accept companion animals," he said. "But there are still a number of small plants that will render anything."[4]

Before 1990 I had never heard of rendering. When my pets died, I usually had the veterinarian dispose of the pets' bodies because I lived in a condominium and I did not have a place to bury them. I always assumed that the veterinary clinic made sure my deceased animal companions were either buried or cremated. When I asked my veterinarian about the disposal of the body, I was told, "Don't worry, we'll take care of it."

Now, I know better—"taking care of it" could include disposal to a rendering plant. Since 1990 when I began investigating the commercial pet food industry, I have communicated with dozens of veterinarians in the United States and Canada to find out what they know about the disposal of euthanized animal companions after the bodies are picked up, usually by dead stock removal companies. Only three veterinarians were aware that the animal carcasses could be going to rendering plants. The rest all assumed that the dead pets were cremated.

Because of the publicity this issue has received in recent years, many more veterinarians are questioning how euthanized pets are being disposed of. Some veterinarians, especially in large states like California, are well aware that pets are going to rendering facilities since this is the cheapest means for shelters to dispose of euthanized cats and dogs. In some cases, pet owners cannot afford to pay for cremation or burial, so they have to leave it up to the shelter.

When I asked Alan Schulman, D.V.M., who works at a veterinary hospital in Los Angeles, about the disposal of euthanized pets, he stated, "In our hospital, the options for owners are to take the remains of their pet for burial at the L.A. pet cemetery, or we utilize Cal Pet Crematory for individual cremations of pets with return of the ashes in an urn to the pet owners."[5] In addition to cats and dogs, Cal Pet also cremates birds and other small animals. Veterinarian Lynn Nelson in Santa Monica, California, stated that about 50% of pet owners she works with want their pets cremated. For the owners who do not want cremation, a company picks up the dead pets once a week from the veterinary clinic and delivers them to a rendering plant.

California shelters I corresponded with had a little different perspective. Most employees at shelters were aware that the company they contracted with trucked the animals to rendering plants. They were aware that few veterinary clinics or shelters have their own cremation facility.

When I asked a sampling of California shelters and veterinary clinics if they could provide me with the names of the disposal companies picking up these animals, most were willing to provide this information. Dead stock removal companies and disposal companies are basically the same, although the dead stock removal operations pick up more dead livestock than companion animals. Nearly all clinics and shelters named the same two companies: D&D Disposal, Inc., owned by West Coast Rendering; and Koefran, Inc., owned by Reno Rendering.

According to a fact sheet published by the National Renderers Association in 2004, animals euthanized at county shelters "are picked up by D&D Disposal, also known as West Coast Rendering, located in Vernon, California. D&D processes hundreds of tons of animal carcasses, tissues, and by-products that would otherwise end up in landfill."[6]

This same fact sheet noted that the majority of animal remains rendered come from hogs, cattle, poultry, and sheep. "Other animal remains, such as butcher scraps, restaurant grease, fish, zoo animals, marine life, and animals from shelters are rendered as well."

D&D Disposal claims that the rendered animal remains become tankage and are shipped to Asia where the tankage is fed to shrimp, eels, and fish. "Sometimes the tankage is used in hog and chicken feed," according to D&D Disposal. If indeed, rendered dogs and cats are fed to hogs, chickens, shrimp, and fish, then we are eating the second-hand remains of our companion animals. (In Chapter One I briefly discuss the connection between human food and the second-hand remains of pets.)

Baker Commodities, Inc., one of the largest rendering companies in the United States with some thirty plants in a dozen states, also renders companion animals. Baker Commodities regularly picks up dead animals from shelters and veterinary clinics. In a news article for the *Eugene Weekly*, an Oregon newspaper, Camilla Mortensen reported that Baker Commodities picked up garbage cans full of dead dogs and cats once or twice a week from Lane County Animal Regulation Authority. Baker Commodities also picked up pet carcasses from local veterinarians and took them to the Baker plant in Washington. When Mortenson asked what happened to the remains of these dogs and cats, the executive vice-president of operations, Dennis Luckey, responded, "It is against our policy to comment on our process."[7]

A rendering plant in San Jose, California, San Jose Tallow, advertises on its web site that the company offers "private cremation services" and even shows photographs of urns that may be used. The web site tag line reads, "As pet owners ourselves, we know how difficult it can be when they pass on. To help preserve the memory of your beloved pets, we offer private cremation services and will return their remains in a wooden urn."

Intrigued that a rendering plant would offer private cremation for animal companions, including horses, I contacted the office manager at San Jose Tallow and asked if the dogs and cats brought to their facility from shelters were in fact cremated or rendered. The company chose not to reply. Then I contacted the Senior Engineer for Environmental Enforcement Agency for San Jose, John Mukhar, and asked if San Jose Tallow had a city license to operate an incinerator. If so, was an incinerator located on their premises? Mukhar replied, "San Jose Tallow is a permitted industrial discharger and according to the inspectors, they do not have an incinerator on that site."[8] He went on to say that San Jose Tallow does collect dead animals that they render.

So, despite San Jose Tallow's website claim offering private cremation services, it appears that cats and dogs are being rendered along with the rest of the animal by-products. Unfortunately, San Jose Tallow refused to respond to my inquiries.

Testing for Cats and Dogs in Pet Food

Clearly, pet food companies deny using rendered animal companions and distance themselves from any connection to this practice. Since 1957 the

Pet Food Institute (PFI) has been the official voice for the pet food industry, representing more than 90% of the pet food manufacturers in the United States. PFI stands by its claim that the nearly thirty pet food companies it represents do not use by-products created from euthanized pets.

At the same time, PFI also lists its "Affiliate Members" on its web site, which include companies that supply ingredients to the pet food companies. Among the members are rendering companies such as Griffin Industries, Darling International, Valley Proteins, and Baker Commodities, Inc.—and we know that Baker Commodities picks up euthanized pets.

However, despite PFI officials' denials of this practice, it is clear to me that pet food manufacturers are either knowingly or unknowingly using dog and cat remains in their food. However, these companies do not conduct any tests to determine the sources of protein used in the meat meal they purchase. And even if pet food manufacturers agreed to test raw meat meal product from rendering companies, it would be difficult to identify the animal source since the DNA is destroyed in the rendering process.

What pet food manufacturers, the PFI, and rendering plants point to as "proof" that they do not use pet carcasses in the food is a test conducted by The Food and Drug Administration's Center for Veterinarian Medicine, (FDA/CVM). The actual tests were conducted in 1998 and 2000, but the results were not released until 2002. I had initially requested the results after the first test in 1998 and continued to request the test results for the next four years. I filed the request under the Freedom of Information Act at least twice before I received the information in 2003, including the laboratory reports. Obviously, the FDA/CVM did not make these results easily available to the public.

The FDA/CVM tested for euthanized cats and dog remains in pet food as part of its study on sodium pentobarbital in pet food, which is discussed in Chapter Five. This government agency stated that it "developed a test to detect dog and cat DNA/PCR (Deoxyribonucleic acid, Polymerase Chain Reaction) in the protein of the dog food."[9] The FDA/CVM noted that all samples from its survey were examined for remains derived from dogs and cats. Their results showed a complete absence of material from euthanized dogs and cats.

However, the test did reveal traces of sodium pentobarbital, a drug commonly used to euthanize cats and dogs. When questioned about *where* the traces of sodium pentobarbital came from, the FDA/CVM explained on its web site that the likely source was "rendered cattle or even horses."

However, in early 2004 an article in *The American Journal of Veterinary Research* shed a different light on this subject. The article, published by the FDA/CVM, revealed what they had actually found. Regarding their online contention that the source of pentobarbital came from horses, the report read, "However, none of the 31 dog food samples examined in our study tested positive for equine derived proteins." The article went on to report, "Cattle are only occasionally euthanized with pentobarbital, and thus are not considered a likely source of pentobarbital in dog food."[10] They concluded, "Although the results of our study narrow the search for the source of pentobarbital, it does not define the source (i.e. species) responsible for the contamination." The FDA/CVM's contradictory conclusions made me very suspicious.

Inadequate Testing

According to the FDA/CVM laboratory notes for the detection of species in the food, the researchers stated, "Weighed out dog food samples at approx. 0.5 gr. per sample."[11] In essence, this was a miniscule amount of dog food tested. These samples would amount to less than 1 to 1 ½ pieces of kibble on which DNA/PCR testing was undertaken. *Basically, the testing by the FDA/CVM was done on less than an eighth of a cup of kibble from a five-pound bag.*

According to Joe Donnenhoffer of Roch Diagnostics, "Suppose you have a large package of food, you cannot perform the PCR test on every piece of food, so you take a sample. If the sample does not contain the contaminated it is not detected."[12] Donnenhoffer is saying that if *any* of the eighth of a cup of kibble did not contain the remains of dogs and cats it would not show up on the DNA/PCR test. In addition, keep in mind that cat and dog remains would be mixed with hundreds of pounds of other waste material from slaughterhouses, restaurants, road kill, zoo animals, and more. One piece of food might contain the remains of dog and cat, and yet other pieces of food in the same lot could contain other animals.

A friend of mine, Gene Weddington, a retired chemist for a large rendering conglomerate in the United States, provided some insight into the rendering operation and the cooking system. He explained: "To understand this better, simply think of it as a system where first in is first out with little blending taking place. If a plant received a large amount of companion animals during one day's operation, it is possible that within the finished product there is a 'core' of almost pure rendered companion animals. This could possibly end up in a pet food account." Weddington prefaced his explanation by stating that he knew of no rendering plant in the United States that segregated companion animals from the rest of the material.[13]

More extensive testing for dog and cat DNA in pet food needs to be conducted in order for pet food companies and renderers to support their claim that there are "no pets in pet food." One inadequate and inconclusive test does not let them off the hook. In addition, testing needs to be conducted on the ground-up matter at rendering plants *before* it is cooked. As explained below, most DNA can be destroyed in the cooking process, making it impossible to truly identify the protein sources.

I am convinced rendering plants are aware of what they are rendering in each particular batch, but they are keeping their practices secret. Because these renderers are not producing material for the human food chain, no independent organization or government agency has questioned what rendering plants are sending to the pet food companies.

Rendering Destroys DNA Evidence

There are many ways that DNA can be destroyed, including microorganisms, freezing, and heating. For example, fungi are particularly destructive to DNA. Fungi or mycotoxins can come from moldy grains used in foods. Grains, particularly corn, are used in most dry, commercial pet foods.

Heat is the primary cause of DNA destruction. One expert in the field of DNA study, Peter Faletra, Ph.D., explains how heat breaks the bonds between the two strands of DNA: "The cells of the organism are degraded by the heat, and that liberates enzymes, called DNAses that eat away the DNA. The cell destroys its own DNA when it is dying."[14]

According to John Carlson, M.D. Ph.D., Tulane University School of Medicine, "Very high temperatures are used to sterilize objects, such as surgical equipment, in machines called autoclaves. While no additional damage is done below 0° Celsius, there is no upper limit for DNA damage by heat. More heat means more destruction, until the level at which DNA has been destroyed. Autoclaves are pressurized devices designed to heat solutions above their boiling point to achieve sterilization, typically run at 121° Celsius (249.8° F.) for 15 minutes, which completely sterilizes solid objects."[15]

The temperatures used for rendering and processing foods would destroy any DNA in the material used for pet food. Standard DNA identification depends on fresh blood samples or other non-degraded tissues. DNA cannot be attained when heat is involved.

In DNA testing for cats and dogs in rendered and processed material there is neither fresh blood nor non-degraded tissues. The rendering process often eliminates the markers for the detection of the substance-in this case cat and dog.

The fact that dogs and cats, or any other animals, are difficult to detect in rendered material was confirmed in personal correspondence with Albert Harper, Ph.D., Director of the Henry C. Lee Institute of Forensic Science. He explained in written correspondence, "I think it would be very highly unlikely that identifiable DNA would survive the prolonged high temperatures associated with the manufacturing process of kibble. It is also highly unlikely that any species-specific antigens would be present either. If the DNA testing you wrote about was conducted prior to heating the meats, then the testing would provide results."[16]

Remember, the FDA/CVM tested about one-eighth cup of bagged kibble. They looked for DNA in material that already had been cooked into kibble. In order to accurately test a rendering company's product for dog and cat DNA, the tests would have to be conducted on raw material obtained from a rendering vat where many ingredients are mixed and ground together *before* cooking. To my knowledge, this kind of testing by a government agency or pet food manufacturer has never been conducted.

It is clear that there are many questions and no definitive answers regarding the FDA/CVM's testing on the dry commercial pet foods. Their published reports lead us to believe that *no dog and cat DNA* was detected in the samples they tested and that we should be satisfied with these results. I am not satisfied with their conclusion and I think the results from this single test are useless.

Rendering Pets in Canada

Rendering euthanized cats and dogs for use in pet food product is also legal in Canada. However, rendering companion animals in Canada is on a much smaller scale than in the United States. In Ontario Province where I reside, a dead-stock removal collector picks up any dead livestock that have died or been killed in the field. Different municipalities also contract with a stock removal collector to pick up any large animals along the roadside as well as companion animals euthanized at veterinary clinics and some shelters. The dead-stock collector then delivers the carcasses to a rendering plant.

The Canadian Ministry keeps records of the dead stock going through the system, but no records are kept on the number of companion animals, road kill, or zoo animals processed. This also applies in the United States. The U.S. Department of Agriculture does not require that records be kept of rendered dogs or cats.

In the 1990s, I was able to confirm that the path of a euthanized pet went from the veterinary clinic to the receiving plant, then to a broker, who found the rendering plant willing to pay the highest price. Finally, the pet carcass ended up at a rendering plant where it was rendered and sold to feed mills and pet food companies.

I contacted the Minister of Agriculture in Quebec where a number of the rendering plants are located. I asked that he confirm the truth of this practice. The Quebec minister wrote, "Dead animals are cooked together with viscera, bones and fats at 115° C. [230° F.] for twenty minutes." Also, "The fur is not removed from dogs and cats."[17]

Nine years after I found out that the euthanized animals from Ontario were being shipped to the Sanimal rendering plant in Quebec, a reporter with Toronto's *Globe and Mail* confirmed this practice in a June 2001 article. Colin Freeze reported, "Quebec rendering giant Sanimal, Inc. recently told its suppliers, including shelters across the province that put down pets, that bowing to consumer sensibilities, it will no longer accept the carcasses of domestic pets."[18]

Philip Lee-Shanok, a reporter from the *Toronto Sun,* reported, "The protein meal is sold to various pet food manufacturers and other animal feed companies." When Lee-Shanok interviewed Sanimal's head of procurement, Mario Couture, about euthanized pets rendered into pet food, he stated, "This food is healthy and good, but some people don't like to see meat meal that contains any pets."[19] (If you read the ingredient descriptions for pet food in Chapter Two, it is doubtful that the food is healthy and good!)

In 2005, Sanimal became part of The Sanimax Group, which included Anamax Rendering of Green Bay, Wisconsin and Bi-Pro Marketing Limited of Guelph, Ontario, Canada, which is the marketing division of The Sanimax Group. In November 2007, I contacted Sanimax and asked if the rendering of companion animals continued or if they had indeed refused to render dogs and cats. Mario Couture, the Rendering Procurement Manage replied, "Sanimal group stopped rendering pets long ago."[20]

Over the years I have learned that when one of these rendering operations ceases, another starts up and carries on. Somebody has to be rendering these thousands of euthanized cats and dogs since it is illegal to dump them in landfills, in large part because the euthanizing drug, sodium pentobarbital, would cause havoc and death among wildlife. (See Chapter Five for more about sodium pentobarbital.)

After I learned that Sanimal, Inc. was no longer accepting companion animals for rendering, I wrote to the Ministry of Agriculture in Quebec and asked, "Are you aware of any other rendering plants in Quebec that accept dogs and cats for rendering?" The reply I received was in French, the official language of Quebec Province. The translation reads, "Here is the establishment that now accepts cats and dogs, Maple Leaf, Inc."[21] Over the years I have contacted Maple Leaf at least five times and as of Fall 2007, they still have chosen not to respond.

In researching Maple Leaf Foods, I found that one of its subsidiaries is Rothsay, a rendering operation with six plants across Canada. Rothsay states in its literature that it does not render companion animals, but that is a standard claim from most rendering plants.

In essence, Maple Leaf Foods produces meat products for human consumption with a subsidiary, Rothsay, that is a rendering plant. Rothsay renders not only meat unfit for human consumption from its food manufacturing plants, but also renders "discarded fat and bone trimmings, meat scraps, entire animal carcasses and used restaurant frying oil."[22] Rothsay collects raw material from "butcher shops, restaurants, supermarkets, farmers, ranchers, poultry processors and others."[23] Rothsay does not state what the "other" sources would be. It follows that Maple Leaf's other subsidiary, Shur Gain Pet Food, becomes a dumping ground for the material from the rendering plant.

So, if *no* rendering plants are willing to admit they render euthanized cats and dogs, then where are all those bodies going? In 2007, I checked with several veterinary clinics in the Canadian city where I live to see what they were doing with deceased cats and dogs. They say they are now sending all the euthanized animals to a crematorium unless the owner requests that the pet be returned to them for private burial. The veterinary clinics had received lots of bad publicity when pet owners learned that dog and cat carcasses ended up at a rendering plant. It is my hope that all veterinarians are checking to be sure the pet carcasses are cremated.

Sparky, a humane society resident,
seems to be saying "take me."
PHOTO: SUMNER FOWLER

5

Sodium Pentobarbital
in Pet Food

Sodium pentobarbital is a barbiturate drug that veterinarians and animal shelters use to euthanize dogs and cats. Some of the brand names that include sodium pentobarbital are Sleepaway, Beuthanasia-D, Euthasol, Euthanasia-6, FP-3, Repose, and Fatal Plus.[1] Federal laws restrict the use of this drug and it can only be administered under the direction of a veterinarian. In euthanasia, a veterinarian administers sodium pentobarbital intravenously, which causes a rapid death with minimal discomfort to the dying animal. Veterinarians consider this to be the most humane method for small animals. Sodium pentobarbital can also be used on cattle and horses.

As I explained in Chapter Four, euthanized cats and dogs can end up in rendering vats along with other questionable material to make meat meal, and meat and bone meal. This can be problematic because sodium pentobarbital used to euthanize most cats and dogs can withstand the heat from rendering. For years, some veterinarians and animal advocates have known about the potential danger of sodium pentobarbital residue in commercial pet food, yet the danger has not been alleviated. The "2000 Report of the American Veterinary Medical Association [AVMA] Panel on Euthanasia," states, "In euthanasia of animals intended for human or animal food, chemical agents that result in tissue residue cannot be used."[2]

The AVMA report also states, "Carbon dioxide is the only chemical currently used in euthanasia of food animals that does not lead to tissue residues."[3] Sodium pentobarbital is listed by the AVMA as a noninhalant pharmaceutical chemical agent, which means it is a chemical agent that leaves a residue in the euthanized animal. Therefore, according to the AVMA, sodium pentobarbital would not be used to euthanize animals intended for food.

Exposure to Sodium Pentobarbital

Since first learning about the danger of sodium pentobarbital in pet food in 1995, I have searched many veterinary journals for more information. Basically, very little information or research is available on this topic. In 1995, three veterinarians from the University of Minnesota conducted an extensive study on the heat stability of sodium pentobarbital. The research concluded that sodium pentobarbital "survived rendering without undergoing degradation."[4] The study pointed to one case in which a dog exhibited pentobarbital toxicosis after eating the thoracic organs of a calf. Even after boiling the liver for twenty minutes, the levels of sodium pentobarbital had not decreased.

In addition, I have found nothing that determines what level of pentobarbital can cause toxicity in a dog or cat. However, a 1998 report on feed safety from the United States Animal Health Association (USAHA), states, "Over the years, CVM [Center for Veterinary Medicine] has received sporadic reports of tolerance to pentobarbital in dogs. In 1996, the CVM developed and validated a method to detect pentobarbital in dry dog food and a preliminary survey of 10 samples found low levels in 2 samples. CVM had collected 75 representative dry dog food samples and were in the process of analyzing these for pentobarbital levels."[5]

I contacted a veterinarian with the FDA/CVM, Sharon Benz, eager to find out the results of these tests. Dr. Benz referred my inquiry to the Public Information Specialist, Linda Grassie. She advised me that the results of this study were to be posted on its website in the spring of 2000. For the next year I checked this site numerous times and contacted FDA/CVM several times, including the FDA Commissioner at that time, Jane Henney, M.D, and still nothing. Finally, Dr. Henney did write back, stating "The study is still ongoing and at this time we cannot estimate a completion date."[6]

Based on veterinarians' reports that pentobarbital was losing its effectiveness when used for euthanasia, CVM officials decided to investigate a plausible theory that the dogs were exposed to pentobarbital through dog food. Perhaps this exposure to pentobarbital in pet food was making the dogs less responsive to pentobarbital when used as a drug. The researchers surmised that pentobarbital was finding its way into commercial pet foods through animals who had been euthanized with pentobarbital and later rendered for "meat meal" in pet food.

In conjunction with this study, the FDA/CVM wanted to determine if pet foods contained rendered remains of dogs and cats.[7] Basically, this was a two-part study examining pet food in stores. In 1998 and again in 2000, scientists from the FDA/CVM purchased dry dog foods from retail outlets near its facilities in Laurel, Maryland.

The FDA/CVM did not make the results of these tests readily available to the public. In May 2001, I filed a request under the Freedom of Information Act (FOIA) asking for the results of the first ten samples of the study, plus the subsequent seventy-five samples tested. In September 2001, after more than two years of waiting, and contacting the FDA/CVM, it posted the results in March 2002.

I found out that the FDA/CVM sampled only dog foods with certain animal-derived ingredients. This included products containing meal and bone meal (MBM), animal digest (AD), animal fat (AF), and beef and bone meal (BBM)—all of which would be derived from euthanized animals. According to the FDA/CVM, "In Survey #1 two different lots for the same formulation were sampled in 37 cases, making up 74 samples. The different lots gave the same results in only 31 of 37 cases."[8] The researchers reasoned there was variation because the composition of the raw material may have varied, even if the formulations did not. Researchers analyzed the samples to determine if pentobarbital was present.

Pet Foods Containing Pentobarbital

In the first survey conducted in 1998, researchers found the presence of pentobarbital in the foods listed below, although the levels of this drug were unknown.

1. Super G—Chunk Style
2. Pet Essentials—Chunk Style
3. America's Choice—Krunchy Kibble
4. Weis Value—Crunchy Dog Food
5. Weis Value—Gravy Style Dog Food

6. Weis Value—High Protein Dog Food
7. Ol' Roy—Meaty Chunks and Gravy
8. Ken-L Ration—Gravy Train Beef, Liver and Bacon Flavor
9. Ken-L Ration—Gravy Train
10. Heinz—Kibbles 'n Bits Jerky
11. Weis Value—Kibbles Variety Mix
12. Kibble Select—Premium Dog Food
13. Nutro—Premium
14. Ol' Roy—Krunchy Bites & Bones
15. Ol' Roy—Premium Formula with Chicken Protein and Rice
16. Ol' Roy—High Performance with Chicken Protein and Rice
17. Trailblazer—Chunk Premium Quality
18. Trailblazer—Bite Size Ration
19. Dad's—Bite Size Meal
20. Weis Value—Chunky and Moist
21. Weis Value—Puppy Food
22. Super G—Chunk Style
23. Richfood—Chunk Style
24. Richfood—Gravy Style Dog Food
25. Heinz—Kibbles 'n Bits Puppy
26. Champ Chunx—Bite Size Dog Food
27. Heinz—Kibbles 'n Bits Lean
28. ProPlan—Beef and Rice Adult
29. ProPlan—Beef and Rice Puppy
30. Reward—Dinner Rounds Dog Food

In the FDA/CVM Survey #2 conducted in December 2000, researchers analyzed only one lot of each formulation. In this second survey, other samples were analyzed to measure how much pentobarbital might be present. Survey #2 did show the levels of sodium pentobarbital in parts per billion (ppb). Parts per billion are considered to be minute amounts of any substance which, through testing methods, can be found in solids and liquids.

1. Old Roy—Puppy Formula, beef flavor, 10.0 ppb.
2. Old Roy—Puppy Formula, chicken and rice, 32.0 ppb.
3. Richfood—High Protein Dog Meal, 3.9 ppb.
4. Weis—Total High Energy Chicken and Rice, 15.0 ppb.
5. Old Roy—Lean Formula, 3.9 ppb.
6. Super G—Gravy Style Dog Food, 4.5 ppb.

7. Super G—Chunk Style Dog Food, 16.4 ppb.
8. Heinz—Kibbles 'n Bits Beefy Bits, 25.1 ppb.
9. Dad's—Bite Size Meal Chicken and Rice, 8.4 ppb.
10. Pet Gold—Master Diet Puppy Formulation, 11.6 ppb.

The FDA/CVM noted that although some pet food formulations did test positive for pentobarbital levels, they might be free of this drug now. Every lot of rendered material is composed of various animal tissues. Therefore, if the animals rendered today are road kill or cattle who have died in the field, there would be no levels of pentobarbital detected. If the rendered material was composed of dogs, cats, cattle, and horses euthanized with pentobarbital, this would be detected in the food.

Also, the FDA has no way to know whether pet food brands that were not sampled had pentobarbital residue. The FDA/CVM admitted in the report that ingredient sources vary geographically. "Feed manufacturers have regional ingredient suppliers and manufacturing facilities. Samples available in a specific geographical region may not reflect the nation as a whole. Ingredient sources for pet foods vary based on such considerations as availability and cost."[9]

I was amazed to learn this study did not include pet food samples from various regions in the United States. I believe this would have provided a more extensive investigation on which pet foods contained pentobarbital. Many of the foods tested are from samples of private label or generic foods. I am sure many consumers, myself included, would rather see more testing done on foods produced by large multinational pet food companies, rather than the smaller, regional outfits.

In the same study the FDA/CVM undertook DNA testing on the same dry commercial dog foods to see if any contained the remains of euthanized dogs and cats. The results of these tests are discussed in Chapter Four.

Additional Findings

The FDA/CVM undertook an assessment of the risk dogs might face if ingesting sodium pentobarbital in pet food. *The Journal of Veterinary Research* describes the testing that was performed on "42 immature (12 week old) Beagles."[10] Dogs were grouped and treated orally as follows for eight weeks:

- Low doses of pentobarbital, 50 mg., 4 males, 4 females.
- Mid-dose pentobarbital, 150 mg., 4 males, 4 females.

- High dose pentobarbital 500 mg., 4 males, 4 females.
- Positive pentobarbital control, 10 mg. per kilogram,
  2 males, 2 females.
- Positive Phenobarbital]control, 10 mg. per kilogram,
  2 males, 2 females.
- Negative control, saline solution, 5 males, 5 females.

At the end of the eight-week study, all 42 pups were destroyed in order to determine the organ weight, and allow for tissue sectioning and histologic evaluation of liver, kidney, small intestines, testes, epididymis, and ovaries.

Dogs who received 150 and 500 mg. pentobarbital once daily for eight weeks had statistically higher liver weights (relative to their bodyweights) than the animals in the control groups. Increased liver weights are associated with the liver's increased production of cytochrome P450 enzymes. Analysis showed that the activity of at least three liver enzymes was statistically greater than that of the controls at doses of approximately 200 mg. pentobarbital per day or greater.[11]

Increased liver enzymes can indicate a serious problem. The liver performs many functions, including filtering poisons and drugs; digestion and formation of proteins, fats, and sugars; manufacturing bile; and assisting in blood clotting, to name a few. The prime symptom that indicates liver disease is jaundice, which presents as yellowing of the skin, mucous membranes, and whites of the eyes. Other symptoms may include lack of appetite, weight loss, depression, vomiting, diarrhea, increased thirst, urination, and an enlarged abdomen. The only way to determine if liver disease is involved is to have a complete workup on the animal, including a liver function test.

The researchers found no statistical difference in relative liver weight or liver enzyme activity between the group receiving 50 mg. pentobarbital per day or none at all in the control group. The researchers also assumed that most dogs would be exposed to no more than four mg./kg. body weight per day, based on the highest level of sodium pentobarbital found in the survey of dog foods.

Study Conclusion

The conclusion of the study is that it is unlikely that a dog consuming dry dog food would experience any adverse effects from the low levels found in these foods, and that these levels are "probably safe." (Keep in mind that our pets eat these foods on a daily basis for many years. This study lasted only eight weeks.) I seriously question the FDA/CVM's claim that this drug is probably safe, especially when veterinarians were finding dogs who were building up a resistance to pentobarbital.

Animal Ark, a no-kill shelter in Minnesota, posed some important questions after FDA/CVM published the results of this test. "The FDA test did not check for possible interactions with other drugs," noted Animal Ark. "They did not test for possible interactions with other common chemicals found in pet foods. The FDA measured a single liver enzyme. They then sought to find the minimal daily dose that did not elevate this enzyme. While it may be true (no one knows) that this enzyme is a good indicator of the overall effect this drug has on the body, it certainly is not the only potential indicator. Clearly, other effects could be occurring that would not be measured by this one enzyme."[12]

The FDA acknowledges that had these levels of drugs been found in human food, an instant recall would have been mandated and production of the food stopped.

Pentobarbital is a drug that should not be allowed in pet food in *any* amount. I contacted Dr. Sundlof once again in January 2001 and asked what steps the FDA/CVM was undertaking to have it removed from commercial pet food. After nearly a year of waiting, Dr. Sundlof wrote back, "This drug is not approved for use in pet food; so it should not be present in these foods. That being said, CVM is not planning to undertake any special enforcement efforts to detect pentobarbital in pet food.[13]

If no action is being taken by the CVM to remove this drug from commercial pet food, then I suggest that every pet food company test its raw material for pentobarbital and if found, they should list it on the label. Pet owners have a right to know if they are feeding a food that contains a euthanizing drug.

Wild Life Consuming Sodium Pentobarbital

Farm animals who are euthanized with sodium pentobarbital must be carefully disposed of because wild animals might eat the euthanized animal. This could cause serious problems. Lori Miser, D.V.M., from the Illinois Department of Agriculture, wrote, "Bald and golden eagles as well as dogs, cats, and a wide variety of zoo animals have died after consuming animal parts from animals euthanized with common euthanasia solutions—secondary sodium pentobarbital toxicosis."[14]

In "Euthanasia of Horses," an information sheet published by the California Department of Food and Agriculture, Animal Health and Food, it is clear that proper disposal of a euthanized carcass is imperative. It warns: "After barbiturate overdoses, the carcass of the horse will be unfit for human or animal consumption. Keep in mind that house pets and wildlife that ingest portions of the barbiturate-injected carcass can be poisoned."[15]

Perhaps the most compelling information on the dangers of sodium pentobarbital comes from the National Euthanasia Registry, a continuing education program of the Raptor Education Foundation. This is a nonprofit organization in Colorado devoted to the education of veterinarians about the dangers involved in large animal euthanasia. Raptors include eagles, hawks, falcons, owls, kites, osprey, and harriers. Many of these birds have been poisoned after eating animals euthanized with sodium pentobarbital. This can happen because ranchers have not buried cattle immediately after death or have buried them in shallow graves. The birds can also be poisoned when shelters dump euthanized dogs and cats in landfill sites and the birds feed on these carcasses. Sodium pentobarbital remains potent in a carcass long after the animal dies.

Raptors are not the only wildlife suffering secondary sodium pentobarbital toxicosis. The National Euthanasia Registry cites a case reported by Terry Grosz, a retired U.S. Fish and Wildlife Service agent. His report states, "A hungry mother grizzly coming out of her den, with two cubs to feed, smelled a decaying carcass and dug down through ten feet of earth to get at the meat. She and her cubs died."[16]

Who is to blame for the deaths of these and other animals who have ingested animals euthanized with sodium pentobarbital? The veterinarian who administers these drugs? The owners of the ranch or veterinary clinic who do not bury or dispose of the carcasses in the proper manner? Or do we hold responsible the pharmaceutical companies that do not have proper warnings on their products?

Ft. Dodge Animal Health is the manufacturer of the euthanasia agent Sleepaway, which was the drug that killed the seven eagles. When the National Euthanasia Registry asked Ft. Dodge Animal Health who should carry the burden of responsibility, the manufacturer officially responded: "It was simply not our responsibility, besides there really wasn't any profit in the drug anyway."[17]

Although these drugs containing sodium pentobarbital provide a humane means of killing an animal, something must be done to prevent sodium pentobarbital from killing other animals who might eat these carcasses.

It seems the only way we can prevent this drug from being passed on to other animals, via rendering or improper burial, is to have all animals who are euthanized with any drugs containing sodium pentobarbital cremated or incinerated. In the case of large animals euthanized with sodium pentobarbital, there must be immediate removal of the body before other animals feed off of the carcasses. Ultimately, I believe the FDA must enforce its regulations regarding sodium pentobarbital.

Long-Term Effects of Sodium Pentobarbital?

We don't know the long-term effects of sodium pentobarbital ingested in small amounts over many years. If indeed, as the FDA confirmed in its study, pentobarbital exists in small quantities in most of the pet foods it tested, and animal companions eat these foods regularly—what might be the adverse effects over years of exposure? Because no long term studies have been undertaken on pets ingesting pentobarbital on a daily basis and no literature exists as to how sodium pentobarbital might interact with other drugs, I consider this drug highly suspect in any dose.

6

Pet Food Regulations

*F*or many years I assumed commercial pet foods, and the ingredients that went into them, were closely regulated by a government body, most likely the Department of Agriculture. Once I began asking questions, I soon learned a very different reality. I was amazed to find out that although on the surface it sounds like this is a well-regulated industry, looks can be deceiving. Basically, pet food manufacturers are self-regulated, selling billions of dollars of pet food every year.

Over the years, I have spoken to many pet owners about the dangers of commercial pet foods. At the beginning of our conversations, every single pet owner was *positive* that the government closely regulates the pet food companies. One pet-supply owner became incensed when I told him that this was an unregulated industry. He was convinced that a government agency *must* have been inspecting every piece of meat and grain put into pet food. There was a time when I believed that, too. Not anymore.

Regulations in the United States

The vast majority of pet food is made in the United States and exported to Canada, Japan, and other international destinations. At first, I assumed that the U.S. Department of Agriculture, Animal and Plant Health Inspection Services (USDA/APHIS) was involved. I found out that this agency only *administers* the Animal Welfare Act, which is legislation regulating minimum standards of humane care and treatment of animals sold into the pet trade, transported commercially, exhibited to the public, and used in research. This agency does not have *any* input into ingredients or regulations as they pertain to commercial pet food.

Next, I contacted the U.S. Department of Agriculture, Food Safety and Inspection Service (USDA/FSIS). (Do not confuse this with the first government agency I contacted, the USDA/APHIS.) I found out the USDA/FSIS's responsibility relates to meat for human consumption only. The USDA/FSIS makes sure that meat and poultry are safe, wholesome, and accurately labeled. This agency has nothing to do with regulating pet food. The USDA itself, only oversees pet food sold *outside* of the United States.

After many inquiries, I eventually learned that there are basically three organizations that have some level of involvement with pet foods sold in the United States. However, keep in mind this involvement may be minimal and barely regulatory. The three organizations are:

- The Food and Drug Administration, Center for Veterinary Medicine (FDA/CVM);
- Association of American Feed Control Officials (AAFCO);
- Pet Food Institute (PFI).

As you read the following explanations, I will keep referring to the organizations as clearly as I can in order to alleviate confusion. This may make your head spin, but it is well worth the read to understand how convoluted, and ineffective, true regulation of pet food is in the United States.

The U.S. Government Agency Regulating Pet Food

My main burning question was: *What entity in the government bureaucracy actually oversees and regulates pet food production in the United States?* Answer: The Food and Drug Administration, Center for Veterinary Medicine (FDA/CVM) based in Washington, D.C., is the main agency for oversight of pet food.

The FDA's regulations apply to food, drugs, medical devices, cosmetics, vaccines, blood products, and radiation-emitting products (cell phones, lasers, microwaves)—all products related to human use. The CVM is a division of the FDA and deals with animal regulations as they apply to dogs and cats. Primarily, the CVM regulates the manufacture and distribution of food additives and drugs for pets. This government organization also oversees labeling and health claims made about a pet food. However, the CVM has no input as to the sources of protein, carbohydrates, or fats used in pet foods.

If your dog or cat becomes ill after eating a pet food manufactured in the United States, can you go to the FDA/CVM and request that this government agency investigate? The answer is, *No*, unless you can provide scientific data that indicates the source of the problem. The FDA/CVM requires chemical analysis of the questionable food, along with veterinary reports, any blood work, urinalysis, and any other medical tests done on your pet. Then, and only then, will the FDA investigate. These requirements can be costly for a consumer who has a complaint about pet food.

The role of the FDA/CVM in overseeing the safety and nutritional value of pet food is explained simply and directly in its "Information for Consumers" bulletin. The FDA/CVM states that under the Federal Food, Drug, and Cosmetic Act, "the Center for Veterinary Medicine is responsible for the regulation of animal drugs, medicated feeds, food additives, and feed ingredients, including pet foods." The bulletin also states, "The Act does require that pet foods, like human foods, be pure and wholesome, contain no harmful or deleterious substances, and be truthfully labeled." [1]

In reality, how much influence does the FDA have with pet food companies to enforce its regulations calling for "pure and wholesome" ingredients in pet foods? The FDA's influence over the quality of pet food is minimal. The ineptness of the FDA's regulations and follow-through was exposed in the huge pet food recall of 2007.

Even before the disastrous 2007 pet food recall, there were signs of the FDA's inability to enforce its own regulations. As in previous recalls, the FDA had no authority to issue an official recall to the public for a particular pet food, even though they knew it was problematic. Instead, the FDA waited for the manufacturers and pet food companies to *voluntarily* recall their products. In the meantime, dogs and cats were dying unnecessarily because trusting consumers thought they were buying a safe pet food.

The FDA/CVM's main authority revolves around verifying health claims made by pet food companies on ingredients labels rather than investigating consumer complaints. Pet food companies are not supposed to make claims that their particular product is for the prevention or treatment of a disease.

For example, in 1990 some pet food manufacturers advertised that their cat food might prevent Feline Urological Syndrome (FUS). At the time, the FDA/CVM challenged this drug claim as false. The FDA/CVM gave the manufacturers ample time to remove bags of pet food with this false claim and change labels, deleting the claim. When some manufacturers did not comply, the FDA and state officials seized hundreds of tons of cat food. One company, whose products were seized, assured the FDA that it would no longer be labeled for the prevention of FUS and sold in the United States. However, once the FDA bans a pet food from the United States, that does not mean the company cannot continue to sell its product with the false claim in other countries without regulations. For starters, the company can keep selling its product in Canada.

Non-government Agencies and Pet Food

The Food and Drug Administration (FDA) works in partnership with the Association of American Feed Control Officials (AAFCO), which is a non-government agency. A representative from the FDA's Center for Veterinary Medicine (CVM) serves on the board of directors of AAFCO.

The AAFCO is a commercial enterprise that attempts to regulate the quality and safety of pet food, but has no regulatory power. According to Rodney Noel, former Chair of the AAFCO, this organization "puts together Model Laws and Regulations. We then encourage the member states to adopt these into their laws. By doing this, these agencies then have the power and responsibility to enforce these laws and regulations. AAFCO on its own cannot enforce any of the models that it produces. It has no regulatory authority. It has no inspectors or laboratories. Any inspection of a pet-food plant is done by a state agency or the FDA."[2]

I questioned some of the AAFCO representatives from various states, trying to determine just *what* they do on a state level. It is apparent that none of these state representatives actually test the raw ingredients to be used in pet food. Robert Hougaard from the Utah Department of Agriculture and Food answered my question this way: "We only test for guaranteed analysis and determine product registration in pet foods or other commercial animal feeds.[3]

David Shang from the Agriculture Department in New Jersey wrote to me explaining, "We check the nutritive values for the product. We do not check the ingredients."[4] Arty Schronce, Georgia Department of Agriculture, responded: "Random samples of ingredients and finished products are screened for pesticides and mycotoxins. Drug screening is done in various livestock feed, but not pet food."[5]

AAFCO and Feed Analysis

One of AAFCO's undertakings is a sample feed program for analysis. This is conducted primarily on livestock feed but may include pet food. Because of financial restraints, most states only test livestock feed. Only eight states out of the fifty that I contacted actually test pet food.

What does AAFCO's analytical testing entail? According to the Department of Agriculture, State of Colorado, their testing includes "protein, fat, fiber, moisture, ash, calcium, phosphorus and salt, which are compared monthly."[6]

If the label states 22% protein, 8% fat, 2.5% fiber, then it must contain those levels. The sources of these proteins, fats, and fiber do not matter. The pet food could contain road kill, zoo animals, or slaughterhouse waste as sources of protein. Fats can be obtained from restaurant fryers or the rendering process, and fiber could include peanut hulls or beet pulp (the residue of the sugar beet harvest). Someone once wrote cynically that these levels of protein, fats, and fiber can be achieved by combining old shoe leather, crankshaft oil, and sawdust.

Another aspect of pet food that AAFCO oversees is the feeding trials. When the label says that a food was made following "AAFCO guidelines" and must past stringent testing, it sounds good until you take a closer look at the AAFCO test guidelines.

For example, a typical feeding trial uses eight dogs over one year of age. All the dogs must be of normal weight and health. Prior to the start of the trial all dogs must pass a physical examination. Their general health, body, and coat are evaluated. At the end of the trial, four blood values are measured and recorded; they include hemoglobin, packed cell volume, serum alkaline phosphates, and serum albumin.

For six months the dogs are only fed the food being tested. In order for the dogs to finish the test, they must not lose more than 15 percent of their body weight. According to AAFCO standards, in order for the test to be valid, six of the eight dogs starting the feeding trial must finish the test. That is the complete criteria for AAFCO feeding trials. (Some pet food companies also conduct their own research or have an independent company test their foods. Such testing is discussed later in this chapter.)

In my opinion, AAFCO's feeding trials are inadequate and limited in scope, oversimplifying the acceptable test results and limiting the feeding trials to only eight dogs. In addition, the feeding trials only last a matter of months and give no indication of how these foods might affect animal companions who eat commercial foods for years. At first glance, AAFCO's involvement sounds impressive, but in fact it means very little in terms of regulating the safety of pet food.

In a nutshell, I found the so-called regulations of the pet food industry in the United States to be complex. For example, animal feed, which includes livestock and pet food, falls under the jurisdiction of the FDA/CVM; however, AAFCO sets the guidelines for the labeling of pet food. In the end, it is up to each state to choose whether or not it will even adopt these guidelines. Bottom line, all of these guidelines are ultimately voluntary.

The Pet Food Institute

The Pet Food Institute (PFI) is the official mouthpiece for pet food manufacturers in the United States and Canada. In order to belong to PFI, you must be a commercial pet food manufacturer. According to PFI's literature, it is "the [pet food] industry's public and media relations resource, representative before the U.S. Congress and state and federal agencies, organizer of seminars and educational programs, sponsor and clearing-house for research, and liaison with other private organizations."

Over the years I have communicated with the executive director of PFI, Duane Ekedahl, and the Vice President of Technical and Regulatory Affairs, Nancy Cook. There is one question I have posed to Ekedahl and Cook on numerous occasions: "Do any of the pet food companies actually test the raw material to see if it contains rendered companion animals?"

I keep asking this question because PFI emphatically denies that any of its members use rendered companion animals in their products. According to a letter I received from Cook, "Please be advised that members of the Pet Food Institute, which represents 95% of the pet food produced in the

United States, have taken steps to assure that no such ingredients are used in their products."[7] However, despite this reassurance, PFI has never outlined what steps have been taken by the pet food companies to assure pet owners that companion animals are not in commercial pet foods.

Interestingly, PFI has a video on its website, "How Pet Food Is Made," starring Jim Humphries, D.V.M. This video was produced in May 2007, just after the pet food recall exploded. The video claims to "answer key questions about pet food." (See www.petfoodinstitute.org)

Naturally, I was anxious to get the answers to key questions about pet food, but unfortunately, even though I watched the video five times, I never did learn how pet food is made or what ingredients are used in these foods. The PFI video did show pictures of fresh meat and whole grains, and if I didn't know differently, I might have believed these are the actual ingredients in pet food. I suggest Humphries follow some of these ingredients from source to finished product.

The video also advises that some "organic" foods and home cooking may not provide a completely balanced diet. In the video, veterinarian Humphries advises that most pet foods out there are now safe. Sadly, this misinformation will mislead many pet owners who *want* to believe everything is okay now. From everything I have learned over the years, this is not the case.

PFI's information sheets assure consumers that the United States Department of Agriculture (USDA) is involved at the federal level. "Pet food is regulated by the Food and Drug Administration (FDA), the states through their feed laws and the Association of American Feed Control Officials (AAFCO), and the U.S. Department of Agriculture (USDA)."[8]

Reassurance from the USDA in Pet Food Regulation?

Wanting reassurance, I decided to contact the USDA to see exactly what they do in pet food regulation. In 2002, I contacted the USDA and inquired what role this government agency played in the regulation of commercial pet foods. Denise Spencer, D.V.M., replied: "The USDA does not regulate pet food manufactured in the U.S.; the FDA has this regulatory authority."[9]

Dr. Spencer did note that pet foods are generally the same for domestic and foreign markets (same food, different packaging) and that her department, the National Center for Import and Export, was only involved in inspecting pet food for export. The level of inspection was limited to checking that the product is free of certain diseases. There are different regulations for different countries regarding pet food ingredients. In updating the third edition of this book, I again went back to the USDA to ascertain if they now had involvement in regulating commercial pet foods as the Pet Food Institute has contended. Vic Powell of the USDA responded to my questions stating, "USDA has no role in overseeing pet food."[10]

Regulations in Canada

I first approached the Canadian Provincial Ministry of Agriculture in 1991 about pet food regulation in Canada. I learned that three government agencies are involved.

- The Canadian Food Inspection Agency regulates the movement of inedible meat products and administers legislation requiring the certification of certain imported pet foods containing animal products.
- Health Canada administers legislation prohibiting unsubstantiated health claims in the advertising and labeling of pet food.
- The Competition Bureau of Industry Canada administers legislation requiring that prepackaged pet foods be labeled with a bilingual common name, metric net quality declaration and dealer name and address.

In addition to the three government organizations, there are two voluntary groups involved with pet foods in Canada. The Pet Food Association of Canada, an industry group, has a voluntary nutritional assurance program. The Canadian Veterinary Medical Association also runs a voluntary standards program that certifies only about 2% of Canadian-produced pet food. Most of these foods are sold in supermarkets. No government organization or voluntary organization actually oversees the raw materials that are being used in pet foods. All Canadian regulations apply only to the labeling and advertising of pet food.

Pet foods imported to Canada must be free of bovine spongiform encephalopathy (BSE), as well as free of foot and mouth disease. Porcine origin foods (pigs and swine) must be free of foot and mouth disease, swine vesicular disease, (a viral disease affecting pigs), African swine fever, and classical swine fever (hog cholera). If the pet food contains poultry products, the product must be free of velogenic Newcastle disease. (This disease is characterized in chickens by lesions in the brain or gastrointestinal tract with mortality rates as high as 90% in susceptible chickens.). Chickens must also be free of pathogenic influenza (fowl plague).

Foods that are considered to be safe, "low-risk" foods in Canada, include, "Cooked, canned, commercially prepared pet food containing animal by-products (bone meal, meat meal, blood meal, rendered animal fats, glue stock, meat, inedible meat)."[11] For pet chews and treats imported from the United States, the only requirement that the Canadian Food Inspection Agency requires is "proof of origin [country of origin]."

Regulations for Export to Europe

Most of the large U.S. pet food companies that have an overseas market also have their own pet food manufacturing facilities in that country. The regulations for pet food exported to Europe are far more stringent than those of other countries. High-risk materials considered unsafe for use in pet foods shipped to Europe include:

(a) All bovine animals, pigs, goats, sheep, solipeds, poultry and all other animals kept for agricultural production, which have died on the farm but were not slaughtered for human consumption, including stillborn and unborn animals;

(b) dead animals not referred to in point (a) but which are designated by the competent authority of the Member State;

(c) animals which are killed in the context of disease control measures either on the farm or in any other place designated by the competent authority;

(d) animal waste including blood originating from animals which show, during the veterinary inspection carried out at the time of slaughtering, clinical signs of disease communicable to man or other animals;

(e) all those parts of an animal slaughtered in the normal way which are not presented for post-mortem inspection, with the exception of hides, skin, hooves, feathers, wool, horns, blood and similar products;

(f) all meat, poultry meat, fish, game and foodstuffs of animal origin which are spoiled and thus present a risk to human and animal health;

(g) animals, fresh meat, poultry meat, fish, game and meat and milk products, imported from third countries, which in the course of the inspection provided for in community legislation fail to comply with the veterinary requirements for their importation into the Community, unless they are re-exported or their import is accepted under restrictions laid down in Community provisions;

(h) without prejudice to instances of emergency slaughtering for reasons of welfare, farm animals which have died in transit;

(i) animal waste containing residues of substances which may pose a danger to human or animal health; milk, meat or products of animal origin rendered unfit for human consumption by the presence of such residues;

(j) fish which show clinical signs of diseases communicable to man or fish.[12]

Regulations in the United Kingdom

In the United Kingdom, the organization that oversees the pet food industry is much like the Pet Food Institute in the United States. The Pet Food Manufacturers' Association (PFMA) represents approximately 95% of the U.K. pet food manufacturing industry and is comprised of fifty-six member companies. Its role is to promote pet food products and responsible pet ownership, represent its members' views to United Kingdom and European Union government departments, and raise standards in the pet food industry.

If you believe PFMA's literature, than the policies in the United Kingdom are much stricter than in other countries. "Member companies only use materials from animal species which are generally accepted in the human food chain," states Alison Walker, spokesperson for PFMA. "This rules out the use of any materials from horses, ponies, whales and other sea mammals, kangaroos and many other species. The pet food industry only uses materials of beef, lamb, poultry and pork origin, fish, shellfish, rabbit and game."[13]

The literature further states that PFMA members use only materials derived from animals who have been inspected and passed as fit for human consumption. Most of the material derived from these animals would be listed on the labels as meat by-products. I questioned PFMA about the pet foods that are imported to the United Kingdom because of the dubious ingredients used in some of these products. Walker stated, "The import certification relates to materials specifically allowed in pet food—e.g., low risk materials or in other words that which is fit for, but not intended for, human consumption."[14] Walker also advised me that it is illegal to use dead companion animals in the manufacture of pet food in the United Kingdom and the rest of Europe. Although this may be true, still, in the United States and Canada there are no regulations that prohibit this material from being used in commercial pet food.

PFMA leaves it to the member companies to operate their own in-house quality assurance programs and feeding trials. Pet food manufacturers in the U.K. are also in charge of testing the incoming raw materials used in their products. Because of the number of United Kingdom cases of bovine spongiform encephalopathy (BSE), also called "mad cow disease," certain materials derived from beef have been banned for use in pet food. This includes the head, spleen, thymus, tonsils, brain, and spinal cord, and the large and small intestines of cows as well as sheep or goats. It is still legal to use pigs in pet foods because there have been no known cases of spongiform encephalopathy in these animals.

Regulations in Japan

As in most countries, the pet food industry in Japan is self-regulated. These self-regulations apply primarily to the labeling of the foods. The label must state if it is made for a dog or cat, the country of origin, the manufacturer, the distributor or importer, and a list of ingredients.

In Japan, fishmeal is the only item mentioned in its regulations for pet food. It simply states that the processing plants for fishmeal can only process this commodity. No other animals, including cattle, pigs, sheep, etc., can be processed at these plants.

The commercial pet food market in Japan has grown enormously in the last fifteen to twenty years. According to *The Japanese Market News,* a publication that provides statistics on various industries in Japan, the Japanese have an estimated ten million dogs and seven million cats as house pets. Japan imports most of its pet food. "Over 90 percent of imports have traditionally come from three countries: the United States, Australia, and Thailand, all three of which have abundant supplies of livestock and seafood [which compose the raw materials for pet food]," reports *The Japanese Market News.*[15]

Interestingly, tastes in pet food appear to mirror a particular culture's eating habits. For example, fish-flavored cat food is preferred in Japan, while chicken-flavored cat food is more popular in Europe and North America. Japanese cats are traditionally fed leftovers, such as fish heads and mashed fish, plus leftover rice; therefore the Japanese assume that fish is a natural diet for felines, when in fact, a fish diet is not good for cats. (See Chapter Eleven, "Cooking for Cats.")

Limited Regulations Internationally

It is clear that there are no government agencies in the United States, Canada, the United Kingdom, or Japan that actually regulate the raw ingredients used in commercial pet foods. The voluntary organizations, AAFCO, and CVMA set standards for the industry, but have no hard and fast enforcement standards. The logos of these organizations, which are displayed on pet food labels, simply mean that the products meet the minimum standard for nutrition—nothing more.

7

Pet Food Manufacturers

*T*he first pet food was made around 1860 by an Ohio electrician, James Spratt. He traveled to England and while there noticed how pet owners fed their dogs leftover biscuits. This piqued his interest. Spratt decided he could concoct a better biscuit for dogs from wheat, vegetables, beet root, and meat. Spratt ended up becoming a long-term resident of England, and sold his Dog Cakes in the United Kingdom until 1890 when a public company bought his formula and began operations in the United States. Spratt continued producing the Dog Cakes in the United Kingdom and his London factory was one of the largest dog food production operations in the world.

Other U.S. firms entered the pet food market in the 1920s using various formulas for dry biscuits and kibble. After World War I, pet food manufacturers introduced canned horse meat for dog food. By 1930, pet food companies introduced canned food and dry meat-meal dog foods, but for the most part, people still fed their pets leftovers from the dinner table. In subsequent years as farm machinery replaced teams of horses, horse meat products became less plentiful, and meat and cereal by-products replaced horse meat as the primary ingredients in pet food.

By the 1960s, a great diversification in the types of pet food flourished. Manufacturers produced dry cat food, many more canned products, and soft-moist products. Various diets, including puppy formulas, "lite" foods, and life-stage diets filled the grocery store shelves, surpassing even cereal products for humans. Slaughterhouses, rendering plants, and cereal producers saw pet foods as the ideal product for their industries' by-products unfit for human consumption.

Today, pet food is a multi-billion dollar industry, and still growing. According to *Euromonitor*, a major market profiler, "Combined U.S. sales of dog and cat food reached a size of $14.3 billion in 2005."[1] Aside from the question of whether most commercial pet foods are healthy for cats and dogs, the industry itself continues to thrive and grow.

The Multinational Pet Food Company Shuffle

Since the massive recall in March 2007, consumers have learned a lot about the pet food industry; primarily that two or three manufacturers produce the majority of food for large private-label pet food companies. In addition, some pet food brands may have been produced by a small company at one time, but later were bought by a multinational food manufacturer, and then sold, and resold in the corporate shuffle of pet food companies.

Menu Foods, Inc., a private-label pet food manufacturer based in Streetsville, Ontario, Canada, produces pet food for an array of pet food companies, including low-end grocery store brands as well as a number of expensive "quality foods." These brands include various labels, such as Ol' Roy, Nutro, Eukanuba, and Iams. The products are sold in the United States, Canada, and Mexico.

American Nutrition, Inc., based in Ogden, Utah is another company that produces a full line of dry, baked, and wet pet foods, and treats for a number of private-label companies as well as their own brands. Atta Boy, Atta Cat, Blue Buffalo, and Natural Balance are some of the foods made by American Nutrition.

Beginning in the 1950s and 1960s, many of the small pet food companies were swallowed up by large multinationals. For many years, Mars, the maker of candy bars, has been one of the largest pet food companies in the world. Mars produces Pedigree dog food, Sheba and Whiskas cat food, and Waltham, which specializes in prescription diets sold primarily in veterinary clinics.

In 1968, Mars, a privately owned corporation, acquired Kal Kan, a company that dates back to 1936 when Clement L. Hirsch founded what was then Dog Town Packing Company.[2] Kal Kan continues to be at the same location in Vernon, California since this acquisition. Prior to that, Kal Kan had established an international presence with the Waltham Center for Pet Nutrition in England in 1965. In 2001, Mars purchased Royal Canin in France, further expanding its international reach and consolidating its lead in the European pet food market. Royal Canin produces a line of dry cat and dog foods; Natural Blend, Sensible Choice, Excel, and Kasco.[3]

Heinz, the ketchup maker, is also well known within the pet food industry. It produces Gravy Train, 9 Lives, Cycle, Kibbles 'n Bits, Reward, and Skippy. In 1996, Heinz acquired two pet food companies, one in Canada and the other in the United States. The Canadian Company, Martin Feed Mill Limited, had operated out of a small town in Ontario for many years producing dog, cat, and livestock feed. Martin produced Techni-Cal and Medi-Cal, and the latter was sold through veterinary clinics. Also in 1996, Heinz acquired Nature's Recipe, a California-based company that produces specialty foods for dogs and cats. Nature's specialties include a hairball formula, a urinary-health diet for cats, and an allergy diet for dogs.

In December 2002, Del Monte, known for its canned fruits and vegetables, acquired the pet food division of Heinz. In addition to the Heinz products mentioned earlier, other Del Monte products include Milk Bone, Jerky Treats, Meow Mix, and Pounce. Del Monte continues to manufacture Ol' Roy wet dog food and Special Kitty formula for Wal-Mart. In 2004, Royal Canin purchased Techni-Cal and Medi-Cal from Heinz, thus divesting Heinz of all interest in pet foods.

In 1999, one of the largest and most unlikely mergers on record took place when Procter & Gamble, makers of consumer products such as Tide, Bold, Vicks, and Puffs, purchased Iams pet food for $2.3 billion. A self-educated animal nutritionist, Paul Iams, had founded his company in 1946, and produced Eukanuba, and Iams dry and canned dog and cat food.

Ralston Purina, the largest pet food manufacturer, made a decision in late 2001 to sell its pet food division to the European multinational corporation Nestlé S.A., based in Switzerland, for a reported $10.3 billion. The company is now known as Nestlé Purina Pet Care Center. (Previous purchases by Nestlé include Carnation in 1985, which owned Friskies. And in 1994, Nestlé purchased the Alpo brand dog food.)

As a part of the sale, Nestlé agreed with the Federal Trade Commission (FTC) stipulation to sell Meow Mix and Alley Cat, (two dry foods made by Purina) to the Boston-based investment firm J.W. Childs Equity Partners II, L.P., which owns the pet supply company Hartz Mountain.[4]

"Ralston's share of the dry cat food market across all channels of distribution is approximately 34%," noted the FTC. "Nestlé has a market share of approximately 11% of the dry cat food market across all channels of distribution...Nestlé also adds Ralston's 28 percent share of the dog food market to the 10 percent it already has."[5] With these takeovers, Nestlé became the dominant pet food company in North America, and the corporate pet food company shuffle continues, with quality and actual ingredients used in their products being driven by the bottom-line concern—profits.

Lawsuits Against Pet Food Manufacturers

Pet owners are rather reluctant to initiate a lawsuit against one of the large pet food companies primarily because of the costs involved and the fact that many of these companies retain law firms just to handle such matters. I sued one of the large companies, Ralston Purina, back in 1992 after my two large dogs became ill after eating their food. I filed my suit in small claims court where a lawyer was not necessary. My claim was for $120 to cover my veterinary bills for one of my dogs. The company offered to settle prior to my filing the claim only if I signed what amounted to a gag order. I refused and proceeded with my complaint. I had letters from veterinarians well-versed in their particular fields who stated the symptoms my dogs displayed were consistent with high levels of minerals in the food; in this case, zinc. I also had an independent lab analyze the pet food and the lab identified dangerously excessive levels of zinc.

I was very surprised to see that Ralston Purina hired two Canadian law firms along with legal counsel from the United States to represent the company in small claims court. As I described in the first edition of *Food Pets Die For,* I lost the case after we had been to court seven times. I lost the case because this company flew in witnesses to testify, and my defense only consisted of written statements from veterinarians, and the results from the independent lab. An independent lawyer who sat through the court proceedings estimated that the pet food company had spent more than $50,000 to defend itself against my small claims court challenge for $120, Canadian.

Since then, I have heard from many people who are convinced that a particular pet food either caused illness or the death of their pet. But unless they can verify through testing or others that have encountered the same problem, a lawsuit is fruitless and costly. Legal fees can quickly drain the resources of plaintiffs who go it alone, and I believe these multi-billion dollar corporations depend on that.

In March 2007, a group of pet owners filed a class action suit against Royal Canin Canada. Janet Grixti, owner of a chocolate lab, Mocha, along with other pet owners who joined the lawsuit, claim that Royal Canin did not test its pet food nor recall it in a timely manner, causing dogs to develop chronic renal failure due to excess levels of Vitamin D in the food. Mocha, as well as the other dogs that survived, will be on medication for the rest of their lives. This lawsuit is pending as the third edition of this book goes to press.

With the 2007 recall of Menu pet foods, consumers have filed hundreds of lawsuits, mainly class action suits, in both the United States and Canada. In these cases, the lawyer(s) only need show that many clients share "common issues," directly linking the pets' illnesses to the recalled pet food brands. The monetary award in such cases is questionable. According to Gordon Gibb, a writer for legal news at LawyersandSettlements.com, "Under U.S. law, pets are classified as property, and while there are provisions for criminal charges if a pet is abused, current civil law only allows pet owners the right to sue for economic damages if a pet is harmed, or dies."[6]

After the huge number of pet illnesses and deaths due to recalled pet food, two states, Illinois and Tennessee, have enacted legislation granting pet owners the right to sue for loss of companionship and reasons other than economic loss. New Jersey is expected to introduce similar legislation in the near future, and no doubt other states will soon follow. At present, a cap of $15,000 would be placed on total damages in Illinois and Tennessee.

In April 2007, the CEO of Menu Foods apologized to pet owners whose pets had fallen ill or died, but just a short time later a team of lawyers hired by Menu began to harass these same people. After lawyers representing pet owners initiated class action law suits, the harassing phone calls came from the insurance adjusters for Menu. These phone calls, which pet owners described as "bullying," were made on weekends in an attempt to have pet owners settle rather than proceed with a court action.

According to reporter Elizabeth Weise, *USA Today*, "U.S. District Judge Noel Hillman in Camden, New Jersey, ordered Menu to have no contact with anyone who believes their animal was injured by its product, unless they had legal representation."[7]

The battles have just begun, but perhaps this will eventually lead to some kind of regulation of pet food companies and manufacturers. We also need changes in the laws that consider our pets nothing more than "property," like a piece of furniture. Hopefully, the massive recall of 2007 will bring about changes in the laws that do little to protect our animal companions and legally devalue their worth as family members.

Pet Food Manufacturers and Veterinarians

We have all taken our pets to the veterinary clinic for one reason or another. Most clinics that I have visited have had the walls lined with various kinds of pet foods, some prescription, some nonprescription. In my opinion, this is unethical unless a veterinarian has training in pet nutrition. Our family physician doesn't display weight loss products in the reception room. Our family doctor doesn't sell food that may stop kidney disease or aid in the treatment of diabetes. So why is this going on in veterinary clinics that do not specialize in nutrition?

Most veterinarians acquire their only knowledge on pet nutrition in elective classes in veterinary school. These classes may only last a few weeks and are often taught by representatives from pet food companies. Hill's, Iams, and Purina are the largest contributors for these veterinary courses. In addition, pet food companies even donate food to the veterinary students for their own companion animals. This practice has become so widespread among pet food companies that the veterinary school at Colorado State University(CSU) made this an agenda item for an Executive Committee meeting in 2000. "Discussion was held on how to handle dealing with pet food companies and their donations of pet food to the university," according to the Executive Committee minutes. "It was agreed to put together a task force to discuss this issue, investigate the possibilities, and make suggestions to the Executive Council on how to work with the numerous pet food companies that want to donate to CSU."[8]

Major pet food companies begin courting the veterinary market when students are in veterinary school. For example, a February 2007 report from the Student Chapter of the American Veterinary Medical Association at the University of Colorado lists the low cost that students pay for bags and cans of Hill's. The money from the sale of this food goes to the Student Chapter, and the food is supplied for free. As an example, students would pay $12.15 for a 25-pound bag of food, and faculty, staff, and residents would pay $14.65. The information sheet also shows how Hill's supports the veterinary students. It reads: "Clubs' Funding, Vet Fest,

Hill's Scholarships, Teaching Technology Fund, Freshman Orientation, Unique Educational Opportunities Fund, Senior Hooding Ceremony, And So Much More !!!"[9]

Nestlé Purina provides scholarships to each of the twenty-seven U.S. veterinary colleges as well as providing "lectures by Purina scientists and other professional experts; monthly product trial coupons; Purina-sponsored Student Representatives; and free educational materials such as veterinary text books, *The Purina Research Report, The Clinical Handbook*, scientific proceedings and informational videos."[10]

Pet food manufacturers also make donations to veterinary schools in Canada. For example, the Iams Company donates both therapeutic and maintenance diets for feline and canine patients as well as other animals at the Ontario Veterinary College at Guelph.

A veterinarian who requested anonymity wrote to me about her experiences during veterinary school: "The pet food companies plied students with free pizza, free pet food, bags, binders, and even purses with the particular company's logo embossed on everything." Pet food companies also hire students to be representatives in order to facilitate information dissemination on particular pet foods to the student body. This former veterinary student also noted that at no time was there ever a course offered on preparing a homemade diet for pets or its possible benefits. If you are lucky enough to have a veterinarian who is versed in how to prepare a homemade diet for your pet, you can bet that he/she acquired this knowledge from independent studies.

A University of Tennessee newsletter clearly shows how some veterinarians make a tidy profit from research they undertake for pet food companies. The newsletter reported in 2006 that a university veterinarian received grants totaling $108,954 from companies such as Walthams (Whiskas, Pedigree, Purina). A colleague also received a sizable amount from the same companies, including $52,092 from Nestlé Purina.[11]

Pet Food Manufacturers and Animal Organizations

In addition to pet food manufacturers' involvement with veterinary schools, they also sponsor dog shows and other pet events. The pet food industry is a major contributor to animal organizations related to the health of pets. For example, over the years Hill's has donated millions of dollars to the American Veterinary Medical Association (AVMA). In December

2003, *The Journal of the American Veterinary Association* reported, "Once again, Hill's Pet Nutrition has stepped up to the plate and pledged major funding for future AVMA Annual Conventions. Over the next five years, Hill's will provide convention sponsorship totaling $1 million; $200,000 per year for the next five years."[12]

In February 2002, Hill's Science Diet signed a wide-ranging agreement with The Humane Society of the United States (HSUS). Hill's agreed to provide "generous financial support to several HSUS programs over the next few years."[13] Among the perks, Hill's will provide participating shelters with free food to feed all the dogs and cats at the shelter. In return, the shelter will purchase, at wholesale price, small bags of Science Diet to give each adopter at the time of adoption.

In addition, The HSUS noted that Hill's will provide $30,000 annually to be earmarked for scholarships, grants, or tuition reimbursements to staff or shelters participating in the Shelter Partners program. This money will allow individuals to attend various HSUS events, including the Humane Society University, The HSUS Pets for Life National Training Center, and Animal Care Expo. Hill's will also be a sponsor of the Animal Care Expo and the lead sponsor of The HSUS Pets for Life National Training Center in Denver.[14]

In 2004, Iams and HSUS's friendly arrangement changed when Iams announced the end of its sponsorship of the HSUS's Pet Fest because of feedback they had received from the sporting dog community. Iams pulled its support because of the anti-hunting position of the HSUS. However, Iams does still support such events as the AKC Master National Hunt Test, AKC National Gun Dog Championship, National Bird Dog Championship, and National German Pointing Dog Championship, among others.

Nestlé Purina, another large contributor to veterinary schools and animal organizations, is involved in providing funds and pet foods to the American Kennel Club. In 2007, Nestlé Purina was named as a "Diamond Benefactor" donating $1,000,000 plus to the American Kennel Club Canine Health Foundation.[15] Nestlé Purina also sponsors seminars, speakers, and luncheons, for organizations such as the American Animal Hospital Association, American College of Veterinary Internal Medicine, American Veterinary Medical Association, World Congress of Veterinary Dermatology, and the Veterinary Emergency Critical Care.

It continually amazes me how pet food companies promote their products, especially through the veterinary profession. Money, perks, and awards await anyone in the profession who is willing to promote a pet food company's products. Of course, this is nothing new in the world of big business and health. Pharmaceutical companies have run rampant with perks offered to medical doctors hoping to influence the use of their drugs. Fortunately, there are efforts to curb this practice, although there is still a long way to go. My hope is that veterinary medicine and nonprofit animal organizations rethink their relationships with pet food companies. Perhaps with consumer pressure, this will happen.

Saffron found a welcoming home with a young girl, Alicia.
This kitten's mother had been found
in a cardboard box on a freeway.
PHOTO: ALICIA MICHELSON

8

Pet Food Recalls

*P*rior to 2007, most consumers had never heard about pet food recalls, or that hundreds of animal companions have died in the past decade because of tainted pet food. Seldom did a pet food recall make headline news, even though since the early 1990s there has been one pet food or pet treat recall every three or four months, on average. Consumers had a huge wake-up call in March 2007 when more than one hundred popular brands of pet foods were recalled. All the major media covered the problems with tainted pet food, which resulted in the deaths of hundreds, possibly thousands, of animal companions. Some 60 million bags and cans of pet food were recalled.

When a pet food causes problems, the company that produces it usually initiates a recall, then reports to the FDA, which launches its own investigation. In the past, recalls have involved mycotoxins in pet food caused by moldy grains or salmonella, a range of closely related bacteria. The 2007 pet food recall was extensive and involved the widespread use of a tainted product. As I wrap up this third edition in spring 2008, there are *still* many unanswered questions about exactly *what* caused so many animals to get sick and die.

This chapter details some of the issues in the 2007 pet food recall, as well as reviews a few previous recalls to give readers a good idea of the ongoing problem with commercially produced pet food—and the likelihood of more recalls in the future.

The 2007 Pet Food Recall

The biggest recall in the history of the pet food industry began in March 2007. Since then, consumer awareness has skyrocketed on any and all products—for pets and humans. It eventually affected more than 100 pet foods and pet treats. For several months, pet food companies had to pull tens-of-thousands of bags and cans of pet food off store shelves.

In addition to pet food recalls, there are now reports of recalls for a variety of pet products, including pet toys containing too much lead, and a dog toothpaste, PetEdge, which may contain diethylene glycol. The web site, "Itchmo: News for Dogs and Cats," at www.itchmo.com, offers free email alerts whenever a pet food recall, pet-related scam, or urgent pet safety news occurs. You may want to sign up to stay informed.

Menu Foods, Inc., based in Ontario, Canada, was the primary manufacturer involved in the 2007 pet food recall. Menu makes many of the private-label pet foods for various pet food companies in the United States, Canada, and Mexico. In mid-February 2007, Menu Foods received the first of six customer reports that its food was making some pets sick. On February 27, Menu began in-house testing of the suspect food, feeding it to between forty and fifty dogs and cats. On March 2, the first of nine animals in the feeding trial died of acute renal failure.

The media reported that Menu first became aware of the problem as early as January 2007, but at that time attributed the animals' illnesses to possibly getting into garbage, or being poisoned by something other than contaminated food. It became clear after the Menu Foods in-house testing that something was very wrong with the company's pet foods.

The *official* recall began on March 16, 2007, when Menu Foods announced it was recalling several lines of its canned and pouch-type foods described as "cuts and gravy style foods." In the following weeks, the public learned this recall involved millions of cans and pouches from ninety-five different pet food brand names, including large retailers' brand names, such as Wal-Mart, Kroger, and Safeway.

On March 18, Menu first advised consumers that the foods were produced at the Menu plants in Emporia, Kansas and Pennsauken, New Jersey between December 3, 2006, and March 6, 2007. That date was later pushed back to November 8, 2006, a month earlier than had first been reported.

On March 22, 2007, an on-line network started by pet owners, the Pet Connection, provided a list of "self-reported numbers of pets that were ill or deceased." The total number of deceased pets up to that point was 460 cats and 309 dogs—and the list was growing every day. Pet food companies reported a much lower death rate to the media, claiming that possibly a dozen or so pets had died as a result of the tainted food.

Other major pet food companies began recalling their food as well. Procter & Gamble, makers of Iams and Eukanuba, recalled forty-three lines of Iams and twenty-five lines of Eukanuba. Nutro, another major pet food company, recalled thirty-four lines of cat food and twenty-two lines of dog food.

Purina also announced a voluntary recall of its Mighty Dog food brand. Shortly after that, Hill's joined the growing list of tainted pet foods by recalling a number of its canned Science Diet kitten and cat foods. Many more foods, both wet and dry, plus pet treats, were recalled in subsequent weeks.

What Tainted the Pet Food?

A year after the 2007 pet food recall began, there are still many unanswered questions regarding the March 2007 recall. When the Menu Foods' animal testing resulted in animals dying in February 2007, wheat gluten was suspected as the cause. In November 2006, Menu had switched gluten suppliers to a Chinese company. The wheat gluten from China was sold to ChemNutra, a broker, which in turn sold it to Menu Pet Foods.

Wheat gluten is a substance much like tofu that pet food manufacturers use to boost the protein level. It is also used as a filler in pet food. Wheat gluten is made by washing dough made from wheat flour in water until the starch is rinsed away, leaving only the gluten. Manufacturers cook and process the gluten in various ways. Wheat gluten has been used for years as a cheap source of protein in many commercial pet foods and had not caused a problem in the past. However, the FDA suspected something had been incorporated into the product that was causing pet illnesses and death.

In March 2007, the Associated Press (AP) reported that scientists at the New York State Food Laboratory had "made a crucial breakthrough in the testing of pet food believed to be responsible for animal deaths across the country. Using sophisticated drug screening panels, that lab determined a banned rodent poison called aminopterin might be killing the household pets."[1] However, the investigators could not state that this was the sole cause of the tainted pet food problems.

Steven Hansen, a veterinary toxicologist, questioned this claim, noting that animals ingesting high levels of aminopterin experience nausea, vomiting, anorexia, stomatititis (inflammation of the oral mucosa), pharyngitis (inflammation of the pharynx), erythrematous rashes (red skin rashes), hyperpigmentation (abnormally increased pigmentation), chills, fever, gastrointestinal hemorrhage, and/or renal failure. The animals sickened by the recalled pet food did not suffer all of these symptoms.

A week later on March 30, Menu Foods and the FDA stated that inspectors found traces of melamine in wheat gluten used in the suspect pet food. Melamine was also found in the urine and kidneys of cats who had died from the contaminated pet food. Melamine is used to manufacture kitchen wear and counter tops, and it is often used as a fertilizer in Asia.

After melamine was identified as the problem, there were no further reports of the rodent poison aminopterin being found in the foods. Although melamine is considered to have low toxicity, there was no research or findings that determined the exact effect melamine has on cats and/or dogs. The lack of documentation made it difficult to determine what a lethal dose of melamine would be.

Xuzhou Anying Biologic Technology Development Company, north of Shanghai, China, was identified as the source of the wheat gluten contaminated with melamine. The Chinese manufacturer shipped the wheat gluten to ChemNutra, a company based in Las Vegas, Nevada. Chem Nutra then shipped this contaminated wheat gluten to a number of pet food companies in the United States and Canada. It is clear that the wheat gluten was not tested by any of the companies along the way—not even the pet food companies that were adding the wheat gluten to the pet foods.

The same day Menu Foods and the FDA stated their findings of melamine in the wheat gluten, Hill's Pet Nutrition, Inc., recalled one of its dry cat foods, Prescription Diet™ m/d™ Feline. This was the first recall of a dry food that contained wheat gluten from the same supplier. Later that same day, Nestlé Purina PetCare Company issued a recall of all sizes and varieties of its Alpo Prime Cuts in Gravy. Each day a variety of pet food companies recalled their pet foods and the recall list just kept growing. Suddenly, informed pet owners were at a loss as to what to feed their pets.

Pet food companies started recalling numerous pet treats along with the pet food; Jerky Treats, Beef Flavor Dog Snacks, Gravy Train Beef

Sticks Dog Snacks, and Pounce Meaty Morsels, all made by Del Monte Pet Products based in San Francisco. On April 5, Sunshine Mills, Inc. a branded and private-label pet food manufacturer located in Red Bay, Alabama, recalled huge quantities of dog biscuits sold through Wal-Mart and various other outlets across the United States. All of these pet food products had been made with imported Chinese wheat gluten.

Just a couple of weeks after the first announcement of a pet food recall, California pet owner Kellie Little noticed that her cat became ill after eating a cat food she thought was safe. She fed her cat a "premium" cat food made by Nutro Products, Inc., which boasts on its web site that the company is "a leader in natural, super premium cat and dog food for over 80 years." At that time, Nutro was not on the recall list. Little said she had purchased the food on March 19, 2007 and had been in contact with Nutro about six times in the previous two weeks to be sure the food was safe. A company representative told Kellie that only the cat food in pouches had been recalled, not the canned cat food.[2]

When Kellie Little took her sick cat to the veterinary clinic, she took her samples of the suspect cat food, which the veterinarians submitted for testing at the University of California Davis School of Veterinary Medicine. The test results found the canned cat foods, Nutro Lamb and Turkey Cutlets, the California Chicken Supreme, and the Chicken Cacciatore *all* tested positive for melamine.

Kellie Little shared these test results with me at the height of the pet food recall as new pet foods were being recalled every day. At the time, I wondered, *How many other foods are out there that are also contaminated and are not on the recall list?* We will never know. Kellie's story is only one of, perhaps, thousands. Fortunately, her cat is slowly recovering with the help of constant veterinary care. But how many animal companions were not so fortunate because pet food companies were slow to respond or simply "believed" their products were safe?

Despite Menu Foods' claim that the wheat gluten was only used at their plants in Kansas and New Jersey, media reports began surfacing that Menu also shipped some of the contaminated wheat gluten to its pet manufacturing plant in Ontario, Canada. On April 9, 2007, this latest news resulted in the recall of Royal Canin's product, Medi-Cal Feline Dissolution Formula, which is only sold through veterinary clinics.

The Pet Connection web site stated that as of May 16, 2007, pet owners reported the deaths of 4,867 pets (2,527 cats and 2,365 dogs). These were not "official statistics" from the FDA, but rather reported by people who claimed they had fed their animal companions one of the recalled foods and the pets subsequently died.

What Did the Pet Food Companies Know and When Did They Know It?

The questions that persisted among many pet owners, especially those whose animal companions died because of this recalled pet food, are these:

- When did Menu Foods first know about the problems with their pet food?
- When was the problem reported to the FDA?
- Did the FDA act immediately?
- Why didn't Menu recall the suspect pet food when owners first started calling the Menu consumer hotline, advising the company that their pets had become ill or died after eating some of the brands Menu produces?
- Did the pet food companies in the United States and Canada where the pet foods were made ever inspect the imported product?

Consumers and government officials wanted answers. On April 12, 2007, U.S. Senator Dick Durbin held Senate hearings on the pet food contamination. On the agenda to be questioned were FDA officials, as well as outside experts from the Pet Food Institute (PFI), Association of American Feed Control Officials (AAFCO), and veterinarians. Senator Durbin wanted them to testify to the current state of the pet food industry. Menu Foods did not send company representatives but instead chose to be represented by Duane Ekedahl, Executive Director of the PFI.

Claudia Kirk, D.V.M., Ph.D., and an Associate Professor in Medicine and Nutrition at the University of Tennessee, and Elizabeth Hodgkins, D.V.M., an author who operates All About Cats Health and Wellness Center in Southern California, were also on the agenda.

Stephen Sundlof, director of the FDA's Center for Veterinary Medicine (FD/CVM), testified that the FDA had inspected only 30% of all pet food plants since 2004. He then admitted that the plant where the contaminated food came from in Emporia, Kansas had never been inspected prior to this recent problem.

Senator Durbin asked Sundlof what the timeline would be for a pet food company to report a problem to the FDA. Sundlof's reply was "immediately." However, Menu waited more than three weeks to report a problem. Sundlof stated that the FDA did not become aware of a problem until March 15, 2007. Shortly after the hearings the media clarified that Menu first noticed a potential problem on February 20, 2007.

When Senator Durbin asked if the FDA had the authority to initiate a recall, Sundlof replied that the FDA did not have any legal authority, and in this case it was the pet food companies that initiated a recall of their foods. Sundlof went on to say it was up to the pet food companies to let the FDA/CVM know if they ran into any safety issues. Sundlof added, "The recall hit very close to home for me, as I have two dogs of my own. At the time that the FDA first learned of the contamination, I was feeding my dogs one of the 'cuts and gravy' dog foods on the recall list."[3] Sundlof did not indicate if his dogs had become ill.

At the Senate hearing, Eric Nelson, AAFCO president, admitted that his organization carries out few inspections because the industry "regulates itself well." The AAFCO has no enforcement powers whatsoever. During the Senate hearing, PFI spokesperson Duane Ekedahl informed the Senate committee, "Pet food has one of the highest consumer confidence ratings of any product in the grocery store today."[4] He assured the Senators, "Pet foods are safe." Then Ekedahl announced the formation of The National Pet Food Commission that would bring together veterinarians, government officials, and toxicology experts to make sure this doesn't happen again. Ekedahl explained that The National Pet Food Commission was organized to "further strengthen industry procedures and safeguards in the light of the recent pet food recalls." He said the commission's two main goals are, "To investigate the cause of the current pet food recall and to recommend steps the industry and government should take to further build on safety and quality standards already in place."[5]

Senator Durbin's response to Ekedahl's testimony: "I'm challenging your term that pet food is highly regulated—there is no AAFCO regulation, no pre-market approval, no regular inspection, only 30% of these plants will be inspected, no penalty if they don't report, no government authority to recall a contaminated product, no mandatory standards—it's hard to conclude that this is a highly regulated product."[6]

I had first learned about the Pet Food Institute in the early 1990s when I began researching the multi-billion dollar pet food industry. Duane

Ekedahl is the mouthpiece for this secretive organization that caters to pet food manufacturers; his job is to make them look good in the public's eye. For instance, when the first edition of *Food Pets Die For* was published in 1997, it was the PFI that advised pet food companies how to do "damage control" when consumers and the media confronted them with questions about their pet food products. So, when I heard his announcement of a special PFI commission, I thought, *How about eliminating the inferior ingredients used in many pet foods, and test all raw materials for source and grade? That would stop the problem.*

As Senator Durbin pointed out, there have been no standards, no government regulations, and very few inspections. I have little confidence these recommendations will make a difference. Despite Ekedahl's reassurances about the newly-formed National Pet Food Commission, I believe it is simply a publicity move to appease the public.

Veterinarian Hodgkins, who also testified at the Senate hearings, has a special page on her web site in which she adamantly refutes many of the claims made by the pet food industry and the PFI, including the one about pet food being highly regulated. She wrote, "The pet food industry is an ineffectively regulated $15 billion industry that produces everything your pet eats, day in day out. This should make you want to know a lot more about what is going into those cans and bags, and into your pet!" (See www.all-about-cats.com "Rebuttal to Pet Food Industry Response to Hearings.")

Just two days before the Senate hearings the media also questioned a report that came to light on April 10, revealing that the Chief Financial Officer of Menu Foods, Mark Wiens, had sold 14,000 shares, nearly half his shares in Menu Foods, for $102,900 in late February. This was approximately three weeks before the announcement of the pet food recall. By April 10, 2007 those shares had dropped in value to $62,440. When questioned about this, Wiens responded, "It's a horrible coincidence, yes."

The United States and Canada were not the only countries to experience pet deaths from contaminated pet foods. South Africa reported at least thirty deaths, all from the ingestion of foods containing corn gluten that also originated in China. Vets Choice and Royal Canin dry dog and cat food were recalled because the corn gluten used in these foods was contaminated with melamine, the same contaminate found in the wheat gluten in the United States.

Deadly Combination of Melamine and Cyanuric Acid

I have asked this question since the beginning of this huge pet food recall: Is melamine solely to blame for the deaths of all these pets? From the time the FDA announced that melamine in the food was the culprit, it made no sense. Melamine alone should not have caused what we saw with this pet food recall. During that time, I often stated in radio interviews that I suspected investigators would find something else in the pet food that contributed to so many animal companions' deaths.

On April 27, 2007, City Television (CTV) in Canada announced that researchers at the University of Guelph in Ontario, Canada, had discovered a chemical reaction that may explain how pets fell ill after eating contaminated pet food. Perry Martos, Ph.D., a research associate at Guelph's Agriculture and Food Laboratory, and his colleagues reported, "We have discovered a dangerous reaction when melamine and cyanuric acid—two contaminants found in the imported wheat gluten used in the pet food—are combined." He went on to explain, "The two chemicals react to form crystals that could block kidney function."[7]

Cyanuric acid is commonly used in pool chlorination. According to David Barboza of the *International Herald Tribune*, "It is common knowledge in the chemical and agriculture industry that for years feed producers in China have quietly and secretly used cyanuric acid to cheat buyers of animal feed."[8] He added, "Chinese feed producers used cyanuric acid because it is even cheaper than melamine and is also high in nitrogen, enabling feed producers to artificially lift the protein reading of feed."

In an interview with *Pet Food Industry Magazine*, Paul Henderson, CEO of Menu Foods, put a different spin on what happened. According to Henderson, melamine is a nitrogen-rich chemical that the Chinese suppliers "surreptitiously added to wheat gluten to make it look higher in protein. Crystallization and washing of melamine generates a considerable amount of wastewater, which is a pollutant if discharged directly into the environment. The waste-water is often concentrated into a solid for easier disposal."[9] This is referred to as "melamine scrap." This scrap is mainly melamine (70%) but contains a significant amount of cyanuric acid. Henderson asserted, "Apparently, the corrupt Chinese manufacturers got too greedy. They went from substituting melamine for protein to substituting the much cheaper melamine scrap for protein and big trouble ensued." Henderson's response gives you an indication of how well the raw material in pet food is tested by the manufacturers—little, if at all.

In early May 2007, another flurry of pet food recalls began. This time the recalls were instigated because the FDA found a number of wet and dry pet foods that had been cross-contaminated. Machinery at the pet food manufacturing companies had not been cleaned after the massive recalls and subsequent products produced at the pet food company were also being contaminated with the melamine substance.

Tracking the Problem to Chinese Manufacturers

Around this same time, new information surfaced about the Chinese company that shipped the contaminated product to the United States. The Chinese manufacturer, Xuzhou Anying, had shipped more than 700 tons of wheat gluten labeled as nonfood products through a third party, the Chinese textile company known as Suzhou Textiles Silk Light—thus preventing inspection by the Chinese government. Representatives of the textile company denied this allegation, stating the company had never exported wheat gluten to the United States. Subsequently, Chinese authorities detained the general manager of Xuzhou Anying.

A delegation of U.S. inspectors traveled to China in order to inspect the plants that shipped the contaminated product to the United States. Upon their arrival in China, the U.S. inspectors found that Xuzhou Anying had been "hastily closed down." The *Los Angeles Times* reported, "Mao, (the owner) himself razed the brick factory—days before the investigators from the U.S. Food and Drug Administration arrived in China on a mission to track down the source of the tainted pet food ingredients."[10] Mao Lijun was arrested shortly after that and the Chinese authorities acknowledged that his business had illegally exported the contaminated product to the U.S. The other company suspected of being involved in the shipment of contaminated wheat gluten, Binzhou Futian Biology Technology Co. Ltd., had also been closed down and all equipment dismantled.

On May 11, 2007, *USA Today* reported that federal officials said the ingredients in the contaminated pet food were actually both wheat flour—not wheat gluten and rice protein concentrate, which were listed. "That had escaped the pet-food makers who thought they bought wheat gluten or rice protein concentrate," noted *USA Today*.[11]

This became one more glaring example of how little many pet food companies oversee the raw ingredients and the suppliers in the pet food industry.

Lawsuits abound as a result of the 2007 pet food recalls. Pet owners are suing numerous corporations involved in the recall, among them Menu Pet Foods, Nutro Products, Royal Canin, Procter & Gamble, Colgate Palmolive, Del Monte Foods, Nestlé U.S.A., and more. On May 16, 2007 the law firm of Meltzman Foreman in Miami, Florida, announced that a nationwide class action suit had been launched against companies and retailers who sold the foods. The lawsuit alleges that pet food companies market their products as wholesome, choice cuts of meat, natural, and complete and balanced diets even though they are fully aware that this food is largely carbohydrates and sugars combined with toxic preservatives and additives with little to no meat at all.

Contaminated Food Spills Over to Human Food

By mid-May 2007, it became clear that pets were not the only ones that might have ingested food containing melamine and melamine derivatives. More than 6,000 hogs, as many as 3 million broiler chickens, and an untold number of fish from at least 60 fish hatcheries and farms had been fed the melamine-contaminated pet food. "But in each case, U.S. officials said there was little risk to human health," according to the FDA.[12]

FDA officials believe the melamine contaminate would have been diluted with other ingredients in the feed, making it less toxic to the hogs, chickens, and fish. It seems government officials based their calculations on guesswork rather than scientific findings to determine how people "might" be affected by this unknown melamine compound.

The FDA inspects only 1.3% of food that is imported to the United States. And even with that bare minimum of inspection, in March 2007 the FDA still found major problems with food imported from China. The FDA detained frozen catfish tainted with illegal veterinary drugs, fresh ginger polluted with pesticides, melon seeds contaminated with a cancer-causing toxin, and filthy dried dates.[13]

Previous Recalls

In 1990, when I began researching the pet food industry, I soon learned about pet food recalls. As I learned more about commercial pet food companies I began to see a pattern evolve, recalls followed by "the corporate shuffle." Tracking who owned what at any given time was always a challenge. It continues to be.

The following are several other examples of pet food recalls in the past fifteen years, prior to the March 2007 recall:

- **In 1995, Nature's Recipe**, a California based company, issued a large recall pulling thousands of tons of dry dog and cat food from the shelves. The foods were contaminated with vomitoxin, a mycotoxin caused by mold in grains. In this case, the wheat was contaminated. Symptoms included vomiting, diarrhea, and loss of appetite. There are no records of pets dying from the foods in this recall. It was estimated that Nature's Recipe lost around $20 million in this recall; however, Nature's Recipe is still in business.

- **In 1996, Martin Feed Mills Limited**, a Canadian company, recalled its pet food, Techni-Cal. Fifteen dogs died because the antibiotic, monensin, was mistakenly mixed into dry dog food. Monensin is used in poultry feed, but can be deadly to dogs, depending on how much they ingest.

  A few years after this recall, Martin Feed Mills Limited was purchased by H.J. Heinz Company of Canada. Heinz sold the company to Del Monte Foods Company in 2002, and in 2004 Del Monte sold the company to Royal Canin. In 2006, the FDA recalled Royal Canin pet food.

- **In 1999, Doane Pet Care** of Nashville, Tennessee recalled fifty-three brands of food contaminated with Aflatoxin B1, another mycotoxin, more toxic than the contaminant in the Nature's Recipe recall. Aflatoxin B1 was attributed to moldy corn that had been used in the dry pet foods manufactured at Doane's plant in Temple, Texas. Symptoms included weight loss, liver damage, lameness, and death. At least thirty dogs died. Doane, which produces Ol' Roy and other pet food brands sold by Wal-Mart, recalled about 1,362,516 bags. Doane produces pet food brands sold by Wal-Mart, including Ol' Roy.

  In 2001, Menu Foods purchased the wet food division of Doane. In 2005, the U.S. operations of Doane were sold to the Ontario Teachers Pension Plan, an organization responsible for administrating pensions for public school teachers in Ontario, Canada. The Pension Plan invests the pension funds in various organizations and is one of Canada's largest investors.

The following year, Mars Inc. of Nashville, Tennessee, purchased Doane Pet Care Enterprises from the Ontario Teachers Pension Plan. Since that recall, Doane has been bought and sold by a number of corporate pet food companies.

- **In late 2005, Diamond Pet Food** in Gaston, South Carolina, recalled eighteen brands of its food. Aflatoxin B1 in the pet food killed more than 100 dogs. Cat food made by Diamond was also recalled although there had been no reports of feline illnesses linked to the foods. Symptoms can take weeks to appear.

FDA inspection reports showed sixteen batches of Diamond pet food manufactured between September 1, and November 30, 2005, over a month before the recall, contained aflatoxin amounts that exceeded the legal level of 20 parts per billion (ppb). One FDA sample contained 376 ppb.[14] Karyn Bischoff, veterinarian toxicologist at Cornell University, stated at the time, "We suspect that dogs have been dying since November, perhaps even October, but it took the perfect storm of circumstances to get the diagnosis."[15]

Aflatoxin B1 can stay in the system for a long period of time. The food in question might have been shipped to more than two-dozen countries. Consumers and kennels remained unaware of the contamination of Diamond pet food, and the number of deaths mounted. No cat foods were involved in this recall.

- **In February 2006, Royal Canin Canada,** a subsidiary of Royal Canin with headquarters in Aimargues, France, issued a statement that the company was recalling four of its veterinary diets due to elevated levels of Vitamin D3. High levels of this vitamin can lead to high calcium blood levels and cause adverse effects.

Since November 2005, Royal Canin had received eight reports of hypercalcemia in dogs. (Hypercalcemia refers to an abnormally high blood concentration of calcium.) If left untreated, hypercalcemia can lead to bone defects, cardiac changes (including abnormal heart rhythm), kidney hypertension, renal failure, and possibly death. As of March 2006, the number of dogs affected increased to twenty-four.

Royal Canin blamed this recall on an error in the vitamin premix added to the foods. Vitamin premixes generally contain higher levels of vitamins than the amount recommended for dogs and cats. Pet food companies use higher levels in order to compensate for vitamin destruction through the heat processing and the extended shelf life of the product. Vitamin D is much more stable than the other vitamins and less likely to be destroyed during food processing and shelf life.

In March 2007, pet owners filed a $50 million class action lawsuit against Royal Canin Canada. The class action lawsuit seeks compensation for people who purchased Royal Canin dog and cat food and outlines 59 products.

- **In June 2006, Simmons Pet Food, Inc.** of Siloam Springs, Arkansas, recalled 6.9 million pounds of canned dog food because enamel can linings were flaking into the food. This food was distributed nationwide to Wal-Mart, Dollar General, and other retail stores. Some of the lines included Ol' Roy, American Fare, Fit and Active, Pot Luck, Fred's Canine Cuisine, and Twin Pet.

The FDA sent a warning letter to Iams on January 8, 2007, regarding an additive in its foods for overweight dogs and cats. Chromium tripicolinate, which is only allowed as a source of supplemental chromium in swine feed, was being used in Eukanuba Veterinary Diets Optimum Weight Control and Restricted-Calorie dry and canned foods for obese dogs and cats. This additive has not been tested for safety in dog and cat foods. At the time this edition went to press in spring 2008, Iams did not have a date by which time the compound would be removed from the foods.

- **February 13, 2007, The Food and Drug Administration (FDA) warned consumers not to use Wild Kitty Cat Food** due to Salmonella contamination. The FDA had collected and analyzed a sample of frozen raw Wild Kitty Cat Food and detected Salmonella, a pathogen, in the sample. Wild Kitty Cat Food, a relatively new company located in Arundel, Maine, is the maker of a number of raw foods for cats. The specific products covered by this warning were chicken and clam recipe, raw duck with clam recipe, and raw tuna with conch recipe.16 Pets with compromised immune systems are particularly at risk from exposure to salmonella.

—

I have no doubts that pet food recalls will continue, given the history of this multi-billion dollar industry. At this point, no brand of pet food is beyond the possibility of being recalled for one reason or another. Just as thousands of people die every year from food-borne illnesses, so do pets from contaminated pet foods.

Increased inspections and regulations across the board need to be established and enforced. Until then, we will continue to see recalls of all kinds. As the *New York Times* reported at the height of the 2007 pet food recall, "The pet food case is also putting China's agricultural exports under greater scrutiny because the country has had a terrible food safety record. In recent years, for instance, China's food safety scandals have involved everything from fake baby milk formulas and soy sauce made from human hair to instances where cuttlefish were soaked in calligraphy ink to improve their color and eels were fed contraceptive pills to make them grow long and slim."[17]

This same article noted, "The link to China has set off concerns among critics of the Food and Drug Administration that ingredients in pet food as well as human food, which are increasingly coming from abroad, are not being adequately screened."

9

Animal Experimentation and Pet Food Companies

*T*hroughout the United States, Canada, the United Kingdom, and many other countries, university laboratories are undertaking experiments on live dogs and cats for a variety of reasons. Among them are corporate pet food companies using animals to test their foods. Many of these experiments are done in complete secrecy to prevent animal rights activists from protesting.

Although many individuals and organizations protest animal experimentation, still, thousands of animals are killed every year in the name of research. In 1992, the federal government passed a law making acts of vandalism in research clinics a federal offense, resulting in a decrease in protests by demonstrators.

The Massachusetts Society for the Prevention of Cruelty to Animals, a national and international leader in animal protection and veterinary medicine, reports that an estimated four million animals per year are used to test the safety of cosmetics, food additives, packing materials, industrial chemicals, and fabric treatments. "This represents about 13 percent of all animals used in U.S. laboratories today," according to the Center for Laboratory Animal Welfare. "The other 87 percent are used in education and in basic biomedical research, including the development of new drugs and vaccines."[1]

About 95% of the four million animals used in testing are mice, rats, guinea pigs, and hamsters. Rabbits, dogs, cats, primates, birds, and fish are also used. There are many examples of animal cruelty among researchers, and thousands of incidences of unnecessary animal experimentation. The following two examples speak volumes about the thousands of ridiculous and unnecessary experiments involving inhumane treatment of animals.

- In a spinal cord injury course at Ohio State University in 2006, a course nicknamed "Cruelty 101," students dropped heavy weights onto the exposed spinal cords of rats and mice and then forced the animals to perform various exercises. "More than 300 neurologists and neurosurgeons have joined Physicians Committee for Responsible Medicine (PCRM) in asking Ohio State University officials to implement alternatives to the class," stated Kristie Stoick from PCRM.[2]

- In February 2007, a whistleblower who worked at the University of Colorado, Denver, Health Science Center, contacted Stop Animal Tests. He reported experiments conducted by Moshe Solomonow, a researcher at the University of Colorado, which involved cutting open the backs of cats down to their spinal cords and attaching "S" hooks to their spinal ligaments. A machine then applied pressure in an effort to approximate what might happen if cats were carrying heavy loads on their backs. This experiment was an attempt to use four-legged animals to study back pain in humans.

Responding to the need for such an experiment, Marius Maxwell, a neurosurgeon, stated, "Dr. Solomonow's experiments are redundant and the applicability to humans is non-existent."[3] For more than fifteen years, this researcher has killed hundreds of cats in these worthless experiments using taxpayers' dollars.

Animal welfare groups have been speaking out against animal experimentation for years, finding ways to protest inhumane and useless mistreatment of animals while educating the general public about the companies and products that benefit from these experiments. A good example of their success is the dramatic decrease in U.S. medical schools' use of live animals for teaching physiology classes. Today, about 90% of medical schools in the United States have given up all animal use in standard courses, according to PCRM. Only eight American schools continue to teach physiology courses by carving up live animals.[4] Thanks to organizations like Doctors Against Lab Dogs, animal experimentation among medical students has largely ended.

Corporate Funding of Cruelty

For years, corporate-owned pet food companies have funded a number of university research facilities that conduct experiments on dogs and cats. Pet food companies defend these experiments as "necessary" in order to find out if certain ingredients (usually cheap ingredients) have an effect on the animals.

Documented animal experimentation by some pet food companies includes surgery, intentionally breaking bones, starvation, forced obesity, deprivation of key nutrients and minerals, induced kidney failure, intentional wounding, and surgical removal of parts of kidneys, livers, intestines, and stomachs. Animals are often killed in order to examine the bodies after an experiment. (Further in this chapter are specific examples of animal experimentation.)

Animals experience untold pain and suffering because pet food companies claim they need more "scientific data" to improve the health of our animal companions. In my opinion, these experiments are unnecessary and inhumane, and only serve the bottom-line profits of corporate pet food interests. From what I can discern, pet food companies carry out invasive procedures on animals under the guise of "health concerns," yet their goal seems to be how will cheap ingredients affect a dog or cat.

If a pet food company wants to find out if a dog or cat will eat a particular food, the company could supply pet owners with the test food, have the owners feed it to their dogs or cats, and collect stool samples. If necessary, pet owners could supply pet food companies with blood samples drawn by pet owners' veterinarians. I look forward to the day when pet food companies stop their in-house food testing on confined cats and dogs and seek more humane alternatives.

Hopefully, this information will motivate consumers to stop buying food from pet food companies that conduct animal experimentation—and demand they change their practices. If enough consumers buy *only* cruelty-free pet food, then perhaps corporate practices will change as profits are affected.

Iams and Animal Experimentation

One pet food company in particular, Iams, has received considerable negative publicity in the last ten years because of the animal experimentation the company has undertaken. *The Sunday Express,* a British newspaper, reported on these atrocities in May 2001. "Our investigation has revealed that hundreds of animals suffered incredible agony in experiments designed to perfect Iams. A huge dossier of research papers exposes how scientists deliberately induced kidney failure and other conditions in dogs and cats. Some experiments involved performing operations on healthy animals that were later killed."[5]

A few years later, two animal rights organizations, In Defense of Animals, based in the United States, and Uncaged Campaigns, based in the United Kingdom, outlined some of Iam's animal experiments. Iams representatives claimed that the company used these studies to support Iams' nutritional claims, which are used to market the company's products. Documented Iams experimentation conducted on dogs and cats included the following examples, and more.

- Twenty-eight cats' bellies were cut to see the effect of feeding them fiber, then the cats were killed. (Bueno, AR, et al, *Nutrition Research,* Vol. 20, No. 9, pp. 1319-1328, 2000.)
- Thirty-one dogs' kidneys were removed to increase the risk of kidney disease, and then they were killed and dissected. (University of Georgia and the Iams Company, Finco, DR, et al, *American Journal of Veterinary Research,* Vol. 55, No. 9, pp. 1282-1290, 1994.)
- Bones in eighteen dogs' front and back legs were cut out and stressed until they broke. (University of Wisconsin and the Iams Company, Crenshaw, TD, et al, *Proceedings of 1998 Iams Nutrition Symposium.)*
- Ten dogs were killed to study the effect of fiber in diets. (Mississippi State University and the Iams Company, Buddington, RK, et al, *American Journal of Veterinary Research,* Vol. 60, No. 3, pp. 354-358, 1999.)
- Eighteen male puppies' kidneys were intentionally chemically damaged; they were fed experimental diets; tubes were inserted in their penises; then the puppies were killed. (Colorado State University and the Iams Company, Grauer, GF, et al, *American Journal of Veterinary Research,* Vol. 57, No. 6, pp. 948-956, 1996.)

- Twenty-eight cats were surgically forced into kidney failure and either died during the experiment or were killed to study the effects of protein. (University of Georgia and the Iams Company, Proceedings of the 1998 Iams Nutrition Symposium.)
- Fifteen dogs' bellies were cut open and tubes attached to their intestines, the contents of which were pumped out every ten minutes for two hours, then the dogs were killed. (University of Nebraska-Lincoln and the Iams Company, Hallman, JE, et al, *Nutrition Research*, Vol. 16, No. 2, pp. 303-313, 1996.)
- Sixteen dogs' bellies were cut open and parts of their intestines taken. (University of Alberta and the Iams Company. *Journal of the American Society of Nutritional Sciences,* 1998.)
- Healthy puppies, chicks, and rats had bone and cartilage removed to study bone and joint development. (Purdue University and the Iams Company, *Proceedings of the 2000 Iams Nutrition Symposium.)*
- Twenty-four cats had their female organs and parts of their livers removed; overfed until they were made obese, and then starved. (University of Kentucky and the Iams Company, Ibrahim, WH, et al, *American Journal of Veterinary Research,* Vol. 61, No. 5, May 2000.)
- Six dogs had tubes implanted into their intestines and fluid drained repeatedly to study cereal flours. (University of Illinois and the Iams Company, Murray, SM, et al, *Journal of Animal Science,* 77, pp. 2180-2186, 1999.)
- Thirty dogs were intentionally wounded, then patches of skin containing the wounds removed to study wound healing. (Auburn University and the Iams Company, Mooney, MA, et al, *American Journal of Veterinary Research,* Vol. 59, No. 7, pp. 859-863, 1998.)
- Parts of twenty-eight dogs' large intestines were removed to study the effects of fiber. (University of Missouri and the Iams Company, Howard, MD, et al, *Journal of Animal Science,* Vol. 75 (Suppl. 1), pp. 136, 1997.)[6]

Procter & Gamble (P&G) purchased Iams in September 1999 and issued a code of ethics, attempting to diffuse some of the bad press about its animal experimentation. Animal People, an on-line organization devoted to the health and welfare of pets, reported that P&G stated its intention to phase out animal testing as fast as alternatives could be developed and approved by regulators. According to P&G, "The new code of ethics reflects the decision made two years ago by Iams to start no further studies which required euthanasia of cats and dogs. It applies to all Iams research in the development of pet food, regardless of whether it is conducted by universities, our own scientists, or others."[7]

Procter & Gamble's code of ethics was short-lived when, in December 2002, its pet food company, Iams, undertook a three-year experiment at the University of Mississippi to test their "Dental Defense" diets. This experiment involved twenty-one beagles who were induced with gingivitis, a painful periodontal disease. Researchers cut the dogs' gums, than sutured them. At the end of the experiment, the dogs were transferred to another research facility.

A representative for People for the Ethical Treatment of Animals (PETA), observed that this is precisely how Iams operates—keeping dogs in cramped cages and conducting invasive tests on them for years on end, and then "adopting" them out to other testing laboratories rather than into loving homes. No wonder Iams has never revealed the location of its "retirement center."[8]

In May 2004, Keep On Fighting, an animal rights organization in the United Kingdom, reported that researchers at Auburn University in Auburn, Alabama, took thirty-two Great Dane puppies, and put them into three groups for a study funded by Iams. "They killed two puppies from each group at 4, 6, and 12 months of age to study the effects of adding calcium and phosphorous to their food," according to a report by Keep on Fighting. "They killed the remaining puppies when they were 18 months old."[9] This happened after a spokesperson for Iams had stated in June 2002 that the company would *never* conduct experiments that would result in the death of any animal.

For nearly ten months in 2002 and early 2003, an investigator with PETA went undercover at an Iams contract-testing laboratory. He videotaped numerous examples of inhumane treatment of animals. He discovered a dark and sordid secret beneath the wholesome image of the dog- and cat-food manufacturer. The web site, IamsCruelty.com, describes the investigator's findings: "Dogs who had gone crazy from intense confinement to barren steel cages and cement cells; live dogs left piled on a filthy paint-chipped floor after having chunks of muscle hacked from their thighs; dogs surgically debarked; and horribly sick dogs and cats languishing in their cages, neglected and left to suffer with no veterinary care."[10]

In March 2007, the Group for the Education of Animal-Related Issues (GEARI), a non-profit educational group, reported that Sinclair Research Center was found guilty of committing nearly forty violations of the Federal Animal Welfare Act and agreed to pay a fine of $33,000. The report concluded, "The gravity of the violations alleged in this complaint is great."[11] GEARI noted that Sinclair Research "is also a licensed dealer of research animals. According to the Agriculture Department, the company sold more than 6,500 animals for a combined revenue of at least $4.5 million from 2001 to 2004."[12]

Iams has gone on the offensive in its recent responses to animal cruelty claims. The pet food company now hosts a web site called "Iams Against Cruelty.com," labeling this site as "a resource dedicated to stopping animal cruelty." This web site says it wants to educate people about P&G animal testing policies and Iams animal research, and "to empower people to report cruel animal testing and animal abuse."[13] To me, it reads like a thinly disguised public relations attempt to gloss over serious claims against Iams and P&G for unnecessary animal experimentation.

In February 2008, I contacted PETA and questioned if Iams' experiments on dogs and cats had stopped. Shalin Gala, Senior Researcher for PETA, replied, "Iams has made some improvements but things are still not right." As an example, "PETA pushed Iams into doing palatability studies in 'volunteers' homes and so far 70% of animals used in Iams' tests are involved in these humane, in-home tests. Unfortunately, other studies are being done in the Iams laboratory instead of in conjunction with veterinarians and their clients as we have requested."[14]

Other Pet Food Companies and Animal Experimentation

Iams is not the only pet food company that undertakes animal experimentation. In 2001, a press release issued by the nonprofit organization, Animal Protection Institute (API), stated, "Other large pet food manufacturers, including Hill's, Waltham's, and Ralston Purina among others, have funded, sponsored or conducted many studies that caused significant pain, discomfort or distress, used invasive procedures and/or resulted in the death of the subject animals."[15]

The Alternative Veterinary Medicine Centre in Oxfordshire, England, stated unequivocally, "Companies like Procter & Gamble are massive animal experimenters. They make many household products with household names. They make Eukanuba and Iams animal foods."

Much of this manufacturing involves animal experiments. Other animal food manufacturers also perform animal experiments. In addition to important nutritional questions, there are ethical questions to address. Many of the most popular brands of pet food (including rabbit, ferret, and bird food) are manufactured involving animal experimentation. Reducing this fact to its essentials, buying such foods is funding meaningless laboratory cruelty. Such research has little or no scientific justification but brings great commercial rewards.

Nestlé Purina kept forty-eight Labrador retrievers in a laboratory environment for fifteen years, unless death occurred. These dogs had their diet restricted for the first three years of the study, "after which their diet was restricted still further until some animals were being fed just half the amount of food as their litter mates," according to the Alternative Veterinary Medicine Centre.[16] Body weight of the feed-restricted dogs was on average 26% lower than the body weight of littermates. This experiment was undertaken to determine the effects of diet restrictions.

The *Journal of Animal Physiology & Animal Nutrition* reported in 2003 that Hill's Pet Nutrition, U.S.A, undertook studies on thirty-six kittens who were housed alone for thirteen weeks, beginning when they were just over nine weeks old. "They were fed a diet designed to stunt their growth, which resulted in normally fed kittens gaining up to 56% more weight per day than kittens in the study. Blood samples were taken from the kittens' jugular veins."[17] The purpose of such cruel treatment was not defined.

In another experiment by Hill's Pet Nutrition, the British Union for the Abolition of Vivisection reported that "42 puppies fed a zinc depleted diet for 2 weeks suffered deficiency symptoms such as crushed plaques on their face and feet, lethargy and anorexia." The report continued, "In a further test, 5 out of one group of 6 puppies kept on a zinc-free diet had to be removed from the test, as their symptoms were so severe. At the end of the test, dew claws, one canine tooth, and testes were removed [surgically] from all puppies for zinc analysis."[18]

In the same report, the British Union for the Abolition of Vivisection also identified Alpo Pet Foods, U.S.A. as a company experimenting on dogs and cats. The report stated, "15 cats, fed until obese, were then starved by only being given completely unpalatable food [called 'voluntary starvation' by researchers]. They lost 26-40% of their body weight and developed severe muscle wasting, dehydration, lethargy, major blood abnormalities and swollen and damaged livers. When finally given normal food, 11 were unable to eat and had to be tube-fed."[19]

Menu Foods and Animal Experimentation

While many consumers are aware of Menu Foods' involvement with the massive pet food recall of 2007, few know that Menu Foods funds animal experimentation. In 2002/2003, PETA sent an undercover investigator into a contract lab that was being used by Iams. This lab also undertook testing for Menu Foods. In the year and a half the PETA investigator worked there she documented a number of cases of inhumane treatment to the dogs and cats at this facility.

Numerous dogs with their legs caught between the bars of slatted cage floors had swollen and inflamed paw pads from walking on the slatted steel floors for months. The investigator videotaped one dog who had such severe injuries that both her hind legs were cut to the bone. "This miserable dog, identified only as (H)8J483, was left to suffer for seven days without any painkillers until the veterinary technicians finally killed her. Her body parts were sold to other companies," reported the PETA investigator.[20] This undercover investigator identified several other cases of abuse in this same facility.

In early 2007, pet owners advised Menu Foods that their dogs and cats were dying after eating foods made by this company. What steps did Menu take to find out why this was happening? They fed the suspect food to a number of animals—no one knows the exact number, and Menu Foods won't say. At least nine animals died from painful kidney failure after eating the suspect food. These animals were forced to eat a contaminated and potentially lethal food when Menu Foods researchers could have easily used other means of testing the products. David Benjamin, Director of PETA Corporate Affairs, noted: "Histological analyses and necropsies of people's animal companions who died after eating the foods should provide ample information in determining the etiology of the contaminant and possible solution to correcting the problem."[21]

In the late 1990s, the Animal Protection Institute (API) began speaking out about the problems with commercial pet foods. At the end of 2007, API joined forces with Born Free USA to advocate for animals. This national nonprofit animal group continues to educate people on the problems with commercial pet foods and pet food manufacturers. In their report, they point to Menu Foods' using animals to test the suspect food during the early days of the 2007 pet food recall. "After the first media reports, Menu quickly changed its story to call these experiments 'taste tests,'" noted a spokesperson with Born Free. "But Menu has done live animal feeding, metabolic energy, palatability, and other tests on dogs and cats for many years. Videotapes reveal the animals' lives in barren metal cages; callous treatment; invasive experiments; and careless cruelty."[22]

Companies that don't use test facilities and instead use in-home feeding trials or analytical testing are listed on the PETA website: www.iamscruelty. com/notTested.asp. The next time you buy pet food, I encourage you to first check PETA's anti-cruelty list for pet food companies that do not conduct animal experimentation. Beyond the quality of food, there is the bigger concern that pet food companies treat animals humanely.

Elmer, a shelter dog, waits for a
second chance with a family.
PHOTO: SUMNER FOWLER

10

Natural Pet Food Companies

Since 1990 I have been preparing home-cooked meals for my animal companions. During this time I have also encountered wonderful veterinarians who recommend cooking homemade diets and avoiding commercial foods. Veterinarians Donald Strombeck, Wendell Belfield, Shawn Messonnier, Richard Pitcairn, Alfred Plechner, and Martin Goldstein are among those leading veterinarians speaking out on this topic and writing books. (See the Resource Section.)

A growing number of veterinarians believe that pets enjoy a much healthier and longer life if we take the time to cook for them. In his book, *Home Prepared Dog and Cat Diets,* Donald Strombeck, D.V.M., writes, "Human beings develop nutritional problems mostly from consuming processed foods rather than ones they prepare themselves. Pet owners control dietary quality and wholesomeness when they prepare their animals' diet themselves."[1]

Alfred Plechner, D.V.M., author of *Pets At Risk: From Allergies to Cancer, Remedies for an Unsuspected Epidemic,* first wrote about pets and food allergies in the 1980s. Plechner recommends simple, home-prepared meals as a good way of determining what foods your animal companion might be allergic to. "One of the early eye-openers for me about food and allergies in pets was related to the quality—or rather, lack of it—of commercial pet food," Plechner writes in his book. "Then, as now, intolerance to these diets is common. Intolerance can show up as violent sickness or chronic

94

problems, and often triggers a hypersensitivity and overreaction to fleas and insect bites, soaps, sprays, and environmental contaminants." Plechner adds, "Many mass-marketed pet foods are loaded with poor-quality ingredients derived from sources far from wholesome."[2]

Unfortunately, the pet food industry and many veterinarians warn pet owners that human food should *never* be fed to cats and dogs. Given all that we understand about the ingredients used in most commercial pet foods, I am astounded that veterinarians will still advise against giving animal companions human food. If the humans are eating healthy and wholesome foods, then it is fine to share these foods with animal companions, with few exceptions. Most human food is fine for cats and dogs provided this food has not been heavily processed or seasoned. My Newfoundland eats everything we do with the exception of shrimp and blackberries, which he refuses.

If you are not able or willing to cook for your animal companions, at least add some whole foods to their diet. Leftover meat or vegetables from your own meals are a good choice, but do not feed them junk food or highly seasoned foods. (See Chapter 14 for foods to absolutely avoid when feeding your dog.) Raw carrots, celery sticks, and apple slices are wholesome, easy treats to have on hand. Whole grain crackers are a favorite of my guys—both the dog and the cat. If you can combine some fresh snacks and family leftovers, along with a pet food that uses human-grade ingredients, your animal companion should be eating well!

The Danger of Additives and Preservatives

In the mid-1970s, pet food began to imitate human food in appearance: Pet food burgers that resemble real hamburger; meatballs in gravy (a concoction described as stew); and the latest, pasta. In order to make the pet food look healthy and delicious, similar to food humans eat, the companies use additives such as dyes, flavor enhancers, humectants, texturizers, and emulsifiers. These "humanized" foods are designed to appeal to owners, not to pets.

Synthetic preservatives approved for use in commercial pet food include butylated hydroxyanisole (BHA) and butylated hydroxytoluene (BHT), propyl gallate, propylene glycol, and ethoxyquin. There is little information available on the toxicity, interactions, or effects these additives might have on pets who are ingesting them on a daily basis. (Human food is barraged with numerous additives as well, and many of these are highly questionable regarding their long-term effects on our health.)

Some pet food companies, primarily the ones selling "natural" foods, are using natural substances to preserve their products—vitamins C and E, and rosemary are the most common. Pet foods preserved naturally do not have an extended shelf-life like most commercial pet foods doused in chemical preservatives; however, they are a much safer food to feed your animal companions. If you are going to feed a commercial food look for one that has a limited amount of additives and preservatives, or none at all.

Researching Pet Food Companies

Over the years many readers have asked if there are commercial foods I might consider feeding my animal companions because, as most readers know, I cook for them. After the pet food recall of 2007, I now have many more concerns about pet food companies, large and small, and where their ingredients come from.

Some pet food companies that claimed they used "all natural ingredients" showed up on the 2007 recall list. One of them was a company I had considered high-quality and safe. This was unnerving, to say the least, and I realized there were many more questions I needed to ask pet food manufacturers. Now, when I interview pet food company representatives I ask numerous questions, such as the following:

- Where do the products in your pet food come from?
- Are any of the ingredients in your pet food imported from China?
- Do you have your own manufacturing plant or does someone else produce the food for you?
- Do you have quality controls to check the products?
- Do you test your products on animals?
- If so, how do you do this?
- Is there any kind of animal experimentation involved when testing your products?

Depending on their answers, this will give me a good idea of whether or not I can personally recommend a certain pet food.

The Problem with Co-Packers

When a pet food company uses a co-packer such as Menu, Diamond, American Nutrition, or Doane, the ingredients used in the foods may be supplied entirely by the co-packer. Some pet food companies that use co-packers supply a few specific ingredients and allow the co-packer to supply the rest. Because co-packers produce foods for many different companies, they can usually obtain ingredients at a lower cost than individual companies.

Natural Balance was a pet food I had recommended in the second edition of *Food Pets Die For*. Unfortunately, I did not ask if they produced all their lines of food. During the 2007 pet food recall, the company recalled a number of its canned foods. These products had been made by American Nutrition and contained contaminated rice protein. Natural Balance representatives claimed they had no knowledge that this was used in their foods. Other well-meaning natural pet food companies faced a similar situation; they were told one thing, and then given something different. This is the danger of not closely controlling and monitoring the ingredients, and ideally, producing the product in the company's own facilities.

In July 2007, Natural Balance issued another voluntary recall, this time for a line of canned dog foods made by Castleberry's of Augusta, Georgia. Castleberry's produces a number of human foods but also made pet foods for Natural Balance. The reason for this recall was suspected botulism contamination. Diamond produces the dry line of foods for Natural Balance.

I contacted Natural Balance at least three times over the summer of 2007 to ask what steps they planned on taking to acquire facilities where they could produce their various lines of food and eliminate co-packers. Natural Balance did not respond.

The 2007 pet food recall involved more than a hundred lines of pet food because Menu Foods had produced most of the products. Menu had purchased large quantities of tainted wheat gluten and rice protein, which were used in numerous foods that Menu packed.

Reputable pet food companies that use co-packers have staff on-site continuously, and the product is inspected and tested at least once every half hour along the line. However, co-packers such as Menu and Diamond also supply some of the ingredients that are used in natural pet food companies' foods. Lines are washed and cleaned after each run, but *still* there can be problems. One natural pet food company I mention in my list of reputable pet food companies was shocked to find the co-packer they used had added ingredients unbeknownst to them. This resulted in the well-meaning natural pet food company having to recall its pet food in 2007.

No Guarantees

I place high importance on pet food companies using quality human-grade food for ingredients. I also find it reassuring when companies use USDA or FDA-approved kitchens to make their pet foods. I consider these far better than pet food made in pet manufacturing facilities that may not have stringent health standards. USDA and FDA kitchens are approved for the preparation of human foods; so all the ingredients used to make products in these kitchens have to meet human-grade standards. Even then, there are no guarantees that pet food will be completely safe. Consider what has been termed the "biggest beef recall" in history, which took place in February 2008. More than 143 million pounds of beef for human consumption were recalled after the Humane Society of the United States secretly videotaped diseased "downer" cows at a slaughterhouse producing meat for human consumption.[3]

Simply, there are no guarantees; however, I do know pet food companies that use natural organic ingredients produced in USDA-approved kitchens are the best choices when considering a commercial pet food.

Another reality of the pet food industry is that pet food companies continue to change ownership, which in turn can completely change the quality of the finished food. I have learned that what may be true today could all change tomorrow.

With that word of caution, I have listed some pet food companies that appear to be making healthy pet food using human-grade ingredients. I have also included a secondary list of pet food companies that are making healthy foods for cats and dogs, but I may have a concern or two, and I mention these concerns. With all of these companies I asked them to confirm that they do not do animal experimentation or harm animals in any way in order to test their products.

I have personally spoken with CEOs or representatives of many of these pet food companies, asking numerous questions about their products and manufacturing practices. I have also emailed the pet food companies with specific questions. In some cases, pet food company representatives were very forthcoming, answering all of my questions.

In other cases, representatives answered some of the questions, but not all of them.

In addition to information I received directly from pet food companies, I relied on my independent research since I have been writing about this industry for more than fifteen years. Also, pet owners contact me regularly with their observations, complaints, and questions about various pet foods, and this consumer input can be very helpful.

A number of companies chose to not answer my questions for this third edition. Some provided insight into their processing procedures, but refused to give details on how the foods were tested—in-home or in one of the many research centers. Others offered a combination of organic, human-grade foods for animal companions, along with foods made by co-packers.

I have listed the companies in alphabetical order, and where needed, I note "My Concerns," explaining any reservations I may have about the company and/or the food. Note that this list most likely is not complete, so consider it a good starting point. I always welcome additional information on high-quality pet foods that are composed of human-grade ingredients.

Recommended Natural Pet Food Companies

Halo, Purely for Pets was started in 1987 by Andi Brown, and is based in Palm Harbor, Florida. Long before most pet owners had any idea about the problems with commercial pet foods, Brown was giving seminars and media interviews promoting holistic health for our animal companions and feeding them natural, human-grade foods. Andi's interest in natural foods for pets began when her cat, Spot, developed a digestive disorder and could not assimilate nutrients properly. Her search for healthy food supplements and a healthy diet for her cat resulted in Spot's recovery as well as Andi's new life passion—providing healthy foods for animal companions.

In 2006, Pegasus Capital Advisors, a private equity fund, became the majority shareholder of Halo with Andi and her partner, Voyko Marx, as minority shareholders. In early 2008, television talk show host, Ellen DeGeneres, also became part owner of Halo.

Halo's canned foods are produced in USDA kitchens, approved for human food production. Halo's line of canned foods, Spot's Stew, does not contain preservatives, artificial flavors, by-products, or fillers. Spot's Stew for dogs, the original recipe, contains chicken, or lamb, along with carrots, celery, green beans, zucchini, and squash. Spot's Stew for cats, original recipe, contains chicken, or chicken and clams, or salmon as protein sources, along with carrots, celery, green beans, zucchini, and squash.

With the shift in ownership, Halo recently began producing a line of dry foods for dogs, pups, and cats. As with the canned Spot's Stew, all are made with quality ingredients including chicken and wild salmon. Halo produces freeze-dried treats such as; Live-A-Little chicken, salmon, cod, or lamb for both dogs and cats. The company also produces vitamin supplements and herbal grooming aids for pets. In addition, Halo produces a food for pet birds, and notes that its dog and cat food is appropriate for "any meat-eating animal."

MY CONCERNS: When I questioned the company if they used co-packers for their dry line of food I received a written response from Alex Beinart: "Are you asking who we have producing it? Who makes it? I can't give out that info on who actually makes it or what the name of the company is; that is proprietary info…sorry."[4]

The Honest Kitchen, based in San Diego, California, was founded in 2002 by Lucy and Charlie Postins. Lucy, a canine nutritionist, began preparing food for her own pets because it was a far healthier choice than commercial food.

The Honest Kitchen foods are the most unique line of healthy pet foods that I have learned about in recent years—all of them are dehydrated raw pet foods. This company has developed a way to offer raw, organic, "people food" that does not require freezers or cooking. The raw meat in the food is dehydrated at temperatures above 120° F. to kill any pathogenic bacteria that may be present. The fruits and vegetables are dried below 104° F. so they are still considered raw. All of Honest Kitchen's foods are made in a FDA-approved, human-food facility in California.

You simply add warm water to re-hydrate the foods before feeding to your cat or dog. Each bag of food will make a little more than four times its weight in fresh food when hydrated. For example, a four-ounce bag of Honest Kitchen pet food equals about one cup of dehydrated food. When hydrated, this packet makes about one pound of fresh food.

Although the mix does not look that appealing in its dehydrated state or in its hydrated state, cats and dogs like this food. The dog food comes in five varieties: Verve, the company's original dehydrated raw dog food; Force, grain-free for dogs with sensitive stomachs and ailments related to glutinous grains; Embark, low-carb and grain-free; Thrive, a low-carb, gluten-free "minimalist" diet for dogs with sensitivities; and Preference, designed as an easy, grain-free base for adding your choice of meat or protein.

The company's first dehydrated raw cat food, Prowl, has a high-protein content and it's grain-free. Honest Kitchen is costly, but it does seem to offer a healthy, safe way to feed your pet raw, human-grade food, especially if you are not going to cook for your animal companions. Keep in mind that by adding warm water to Honest Kitchen's dehydrated foods, you are doubling the volume of food, which does ease the initial sticker shock.

Honest Kitchen also has a line of supplements and treats with names like Smooches, Nuzzles, and Ice Pups, made with ingredients like turkey, chicken, asparagus, watercress, dandelion, honey and parsley. With the treats, you add warm water and freeze into bite size portions. If you can afford it, I recommend trying these foods. The dehydrated packets are also great when you're traveling with your animal companions and you need to feed them a healthy, hassle-free, and light-to-pack meal.

Mulligan Stew™ Pet Food, is a relatively new company, founded by Kevin Meehan, a naturopath and biochemist based in Jackson Hole, Wyoming. Mulligan Stew comes in four flavors for dogs; beef, chicken, turkey and salmon. Brown rice is added for vitamins, minerals, anti-oxidants and fiber. Two items seldom found in other pet foods, cabbage and horseradish, provide powerful enzymes that play a significant role in "scavenging the body for free radicals," according to Meehan. Their website states, "Our unique patent-pending formula aids in increasing the presence of certain enzymes that are believed to prevent cell damage from harmful oxidation. The resulting preservation of DNA leads to a healthier aging process and greater life expectancy."[5]

MY CONCERNS: In April 2007 in the midst of the pet food recall, Mulligan Stew™ contacted me and sent some samples. Shortly before the samples arrived I received an e-mail advising me to discard the product because the company had just learned that their co-packer, American Nutrition, might have added rice protein containing melamine—unbeknownst to the company. Mulligan Stew's owner was unaware that rice protein, which was not part of the requested ingredient mix, was being added to the food.

Since then, this company has revised its protocol and will monitor and supervise the manufacturing process. Signed affidavits by both a company officer and the manufacturer's company officer guarantee the raw material used in the foods. As of this printing, Mulligan Stew is still using American Nutrition to manufacturer its foods.

Natura Pet Products was founded in 1989 by John and Ann Rademakers, and Peter Atkins in Santa Clara, California. Natura produces several lines of cat and dog food (and ferret food) that come canned or dry. The Innova line is for both dogs and cats, and the age range is from puppy and kitten to senior diet. Innova includes meat, dairy, vegetables, fruit and grains, along with essential fatty acids and oils. Karma Organic Food for Dogs is a dry food (or dog treats) made with 95% organic, human-grade ingredients. The Evo line of dog and cat food has a high-protein content, along with raw fruits and vegetables, and is completely grain-free. Natura's product, California Natural dry, is a hypoallergenic pet food. Natura claims this food "has the shortest list of ingredients of any pet food on the market;" there is one protein source, one fat, and one carbohydrate, most likely eliminating allergy problems your pet may have.

Other Natura brands include HealthWise, a dry food made with oatmeal and a protein source. A line of dog and puppy biscuits called Mother Nature are made with human-grade ingredients such as free-range chicken and organic grains, and given enticing names like Carrot Cake Recipe, Honey Glazed Chicken, Beef Stew, and Peanut & Butter Recipe.

In mid-summer 2007, I learned that Natura was using Menu Foods to produce their canned foods. I contacted Peter Atkins, a co-owner of Natura, to obtain more information. Mr. Atkins clarified Natura's situation, especially in light of the 2007 pet food recall: "Our products are made exclusively in their [Menu] South Dakota facility [which was not implicated in the recall]. It is important for you to know that Natura has publicly announced that we are engaged in a project to either buy an existing canned-food manufacturing plant or to build one ourselves. We hope to have this done within a year, quicker if we buy an existing facility, possibly longer if we build one."[3] This is encouraging.

I still consider Natura to be a high-quality food, however, keep in mind that this company is in transition with where and how it will produce the canned foods.

Newman's Own® Organics was launched in 1993 by Nell Newman, daughter of Paul Newman and Joanne Woodward. The Newmans have always had animal companions in their home and Nell was very aware of health problems with cats and dogs related to poor nutrition. She wanted to launch a pet food company that provides a nutritious, organic alternative for pet owners. In addition, Paul and Nell Newman decided to donate all of the charity money generated by the sale of the pet food to organizations that support animals' well-being.

All of the foods contain certified organic vegetables and grains. The products do not contain antibiotics, hormones, chemical ingredients or artificial preservatives, colors, or additives. The prime sources of protein in both their dog and cat foods are organic chicken, turkey, and whitefish, all raised without hormones, antibiotics, or chemicals. Grains include organic barley, soybean meal, brown rice, oats and millet. Vegetables include peas, carrots, cranberries, sweet potatoes, and spinach.

Newman's Own® Organics looks like a quality food. They are also on People for the Ethical Treatment of Animals' (PETA) list of pet food companies that are free of animal experimentation. In late June 2007, I contacted the company and asked if Newman's Own® is made in its own facilities or are other companies involved in the manufacture of the food. A short time later I received a reply from Phillips Brown, D.V.M., corporate veterinarian. He advised, "We work with manufacturers that are top flight with the highest current Good Manufacturing Practices standards set by the government that cover all aspects of quality control of manufacturing and sourcing of ingredients. Our V.P. of Technical Services visits each facility, inspects it, reviews all documents, and verifies all procedures to insure that the manufacturers are doing what they say."[6]

MY CONCERNS: This appears to be a very good product, but Dr. Brown did not reveal the name of the manufacturer(s) they use to make their pet food product. This company stayed clear of the 2007 pet food recall, so it seems the company uses quality manufacturers to produce a quality product.

Old Mother Hubbard® was started in 1926 by the A. Hubbard and Sons Bakery in Gloucester, Massachusetts, producing dog biscuits. In 1961, Jim Scott, Sr., an animal nutritionist, purchased the company and eventually moved it to Lowell, Massachusetts. Jim began using 100% human-grade ingredients such as boneless chicken, cheddar cheese, New Zealand lamb, apples, carrots, sweet potatoes, and more.

The company produces the Old Mother Hubbard® line of baked dog biscuits, gourmet treats, and Wellness®, which includes a line of both canned and dry foods for dogs and cats. The main ingredients include hormone-free deboned chicken, ocean whitefish, ground whole barley, sweet potatoes, and carrots. They add cranberries and blueberries to the cat food to provide proper urinary tract health. Their latest product, New Wellness® Core™ Dog Ocean Formula is a fish-based, high-protein dry dog food that is grain-free.

None of the foods contain animal by-products, wheat, corn, soybeans, eggs, animal fat, dairy products, artificial preservatives, sugar, artificial colors, flavors, or dyes—all of which may cause allergies in dogs and cats in addition to being unhealthy. Wellness® now produces a grain-free diet for dogs and cats with five high-quality meat sources. The CEO of the company, Deborah Ellinger, was more than willing to answer any and all questions I had regarding the products.

Orijen Pet Foods was started in 1975 by Peter Muhlenfled from Morinville, Alberta, Canada. This line of pet food is made by Champion Petfoods Ltd., which is a family-owned and operated pet food company. Unlike many pet food manufacturers, Champion has its own manufacturing facility based in Alberta. The company ships Orijen to forty-five countries worldwide.

Orijen is high in protein, low in carbohydrates, and grain-free. "The metabolism of cats and dogs is naturally evolved to operate on a largely carnivorous diet," states Orijen on its web site. They call their food "biologically appropriate" because it is comprised of 70% human-grade meat, and 30% fruit, vegetables, and botanicals such as fenugreek, calendula, marshmallow root, and milk thistle. There are no grains in Orijen pet food.

This line of pet food includes special formulas for pups, large pups, adult, and senior dogs. Orijen also has a fish diet for dogs and cats that contains Canadian salmon, northern lake whitefish, lake trout, walleye, fresh water cod, and herring.

MY CONCERNS: The one concern I had with this company is that in 2003 Champion Foods manufactured dry food for a company, Pet Pantry, based in Carson City, Nevada, which may have contained the remains of a BSE infected cow. The product was recalled. If

Champion Foods used inferior products when manufacturing a food for another company, can we be assured that they are using quality ingredients in their own line of foods?

I wrote to Champion with several questions. Peter Muhlenfled, who shares managerial duties with his father at Champion, answered my questions about Orijen and Acana lines of pet foods. I questioned if their foods were co-packed. He replied, "All our products are made in our own facilities and none are contracted out—ever."[8] This is one of only a few companies that actually does make the foods in their own facilities.

Petcurean Pet Nutrition is a privately owned pet food company based in British Columbia, Canada. Petcurean began as a small company producing one line of dry dog and cat food in 1999. The company uses a slow, steam-cooked process at low temperatures (194° F. and 60° C.) with small batches of food, using human-grade food. The company now produces Go! Natural, Summit, and Now, which is a grain-free diet for dogs and cats in both canned and dry formulas.

Ingredients include turkey, duck, and salmon, as well as vegetables, fruit and oils rich in fatty acids. Petcurean says it does not use meat meals, by-product meals, or animal fats, and is 100% render-free. Petcurean states in its literature that all meat protein, excluding lamb, is sourced from North America while the lamb they use is from New Zealand. The grains, cereals, fruits, and vegetables are sourced in North America with the exception of potatoes, which come from Holland.

MY CONCERNS: I contacted Petcurean and again, asked about co-packing. Their response was, "Information regarding the name of the plant is proprietary due to contractual obligations."[9] According to their website, "Petcurean dry foods and treats are produced at plants in Alberta, British Columbia and Ontario, Canada. Our canned foods are produced at plants in Ontario and New Jersey." Although not confirmed by Petcurean, Menu produces food in both Ontario and New Jersey; however, no Petcurean products were involved in the 2007 Menu Foods recall.

Petcurean's Go! Natural was the subject of a recall in 2003 after the company received complaints of pet illnesses and seven dog deaths associated with one batch of food made by Merrick Pet Food in Hereford, Texas. The recall involved less than a hundred bags of food. After that incident, Petcurean stopped using the Texas co-packer.

PetGuard, located in Green Cove Springs, Florida, has been operated by the Sherman family since 1979. The company's basic philosophy is to provide natural and organic ingredients for healthier animal companions as well as for a healthier environment. PetGuard uses only natural and certified organic ingredients in its canned and dry food for cats and dogs.

Ingredients include human-grade beef, pesticide-free grains, and natural preservatives. Pet Guard Vegetarian Organic dry dog food contains the following organic grains; quinoa, oatmeal, ground barley, and brown rice, plus a variety of organic vegetables and herbs. All minerals used in this food are chelated, which increases the bioavailability, allowing more minerals to be absorbed into the system. There are no by-products, fillers, artificial colors, or preservatives in PetGuard's food.

On PetGuard's web site, the company states it only uses USDA-certified organic ingredients, and defines "organic" as "environment-friendly farming methods using no artificial pesticides, fertilizers or chemicals...." PetGuard also produces a line of supplements and grooming products for dogs and cats.

Solid Gold has been a well-known pet food company since its inception in 1974. The founder of the company, Sissy Harrington-McGill, developed a pet food formula using natural ingredients. This company's first product, Hund-n-Flocken adult dog food, is the mainstay of Solid Gold's pet food line. Other dry foods include Holistique Blendz Adult Dog (fish); Just a Wee Bit Adult for small breeds made with bison; Millennia beef and barley; WolfCub puppy food; and WolfKing adult food, both made with bison. Katz-n-Flocken is a lamb-based dry food for cats.

Solid Gold also produces three canned foods for cats and three canned foods for dogs, along with treats and supplements. Only USDA-choice meats are used in the foods. The company uses foil barrier packaging for all dry foods, which means they don't have to use chemical preservatives or flavor enhancers. Chemical preservatives are never used in Solid Gold Foods.

Solid Gold is a company that I have recommended for several years based on the ingredients they use and the testing they undertake on the raw materials right through to the finished product. The canned line of Solid Gold is produced by Merrick, "but we are in the process of changing to another cannery," according to Leasa Greer, a spokesperson for Solid Gold. "Our dry foods are made by

Diamond."[4] Solid Gold oversees the production of their foods at the Diamond plant.

Timberwolf Organics, Inc., located in Windermere, Florida has been in business since 1998. Its founder and president, Mark Heyward, saw a need for a unique pet food that was carnivore-specific with high levels of animal-based amino acids, but also included multiple grains, fruits, vegetables, seeds, and herbs. Timberwolf makes a line of dry dog foods, one canned food, and one dry food for cats.

The lamb used in this company's foods comes from New Zealand and raised for human consumption. The chicken is also raised for human consumption. This pet food seems to be a high-quality, organic product, free of animal experimentation, and one worth mentioning. None of Timberwolf's products were on the 2007 recall list.

MY CONCERNS: I asked a company representative if their meats were from human-grade meat packers and if any of their products were co-packed, meaning some or all of their lines were actually produced by another company. Joseph Carey from Timberwolf replied to my query: "Due to contractual obligations already in place before the recall, we are not at liberty to divulge this information as it is proprietary in nature."[7] When I hear things like this, I wonder if the company uses a questionable co-packer. Carey went on the say that they use only top-quality ingredients from USDA-inspected suppliers and that the ingredients are as fresh as possible.

Imported Vitamins and Supplements

Some of the ingredients used in commercial pet foods, primarily vitamins and minerals, are not made in the United States. I spoke at length about this with the CEO of Old Mother Hubbard, Deborah Ellinger. She pointed out that there is no source in the U.S. for vitamin C, and she knew of no pet food company, including Old Mother Hubbard, that did not get their vitamin C from China.

Jim Johnson, a journalist for the *Seattle Times*, reported, "In less than a decade, China has captured 90 percent of the U.S. market for vitamin C, driving almost everyone else out of business."[10] Johnson points out that the Chinese pharmaceutical companies have also taken over much of the world market in the production of antibiotics, analgesics, enzymes, and primary amino acids, "as well as the bulk of vitamins A, B12, C, and E."

According to the *Pet Food Industry Newsletter*, "China is a primary source for some B vitamins and amino acids, including taurine, which is used in cat foods." Many companies are now adding taurine to dog foods.[11] Although pet food companies may tell you the source of their vitamins, minerals, and amino acids is the United States, there is a very good chance that the raw material used to produce these supplements comes from China.

China also supplies about 8% of the United States' wheat gluten, used in both pet food and human food. For example, Del Monte purchased wheat gluten for use in both human food and pet food. Subsequently, Del Monte issued a recall of some pet food lines they produced, including Jerky Treats, Gravy Train, Beef Sticks, Pounce, Ol'Roy treats, and Happy Tails snacks. A Del Monte representative stated, "The melamine-tainted wheat gluten used in several of its recalled pet food products was supplied as a 'food grade' additive, raising the likelihood that contaminated wheat gluten might have entered the human food supply."[12]

Disclaimer

In truth, the only way you will be sure of what your animal companion is eating is by making the food yourself. And even then, you will need to use quality, human-grade foods, such as organic meats, vegetables, fruits, and grains. If you eat well, then chances are you will choose healthy foods for your pets. If you're ready to start cooking for your cat or dog, read on. The following chapters offer some good simple recipes, and a few things to watch for.

11

Cooking for Cats

*F*or nearly twenty years I have fed my cats a homemade diet. My cats have all lived well into their twenties, and died of old age. I have to shake my head in disbelief when I read articles or news reports quoting veterinarians who claim feeding your cats and dogs home-cooked meals is harmful. This simply is not true. With a little bit of preparation and a basic understanding of what your companion animal requires nutritionally, you can help your cat and/or dog live a long and healthy life.

In this chapter, I will talk about specific diet concerns for cats, including vitamins and minerals. This does not have to be complicated even though there are many books and articles that would have you believe otherwise. My approach to cooking for my cats and dogs is to keep it *simple*, using the freshest and most natural ingredients affordable. In Chapter Twelve, there are recipes for preparing a homemade diet for cats, including the recipes I have used over the years.

Protein

Cats are carnivores. That means they are flesh-eating animals and require a certain amount of amino acids derived from eating animal protein. Cats have evolved as hunters of other animals in keeping with their nature as meat-eaters. If you are a vegetarian and you want your cat to be a vegetarian, I encourage you to keep reading this chapter, even though you may think this is meat-eating propaganda. There are some serious nutritional considerations for your cat, especially about sources of protein and essential fatty acids.

The primary purpose of protein is to build body tissue and provide energy. Cats need the amino acids that are included in animal protein. Researchers have identified twenty-three amino acids that cats require and a deficiency in any of these amino acids can cause health problems. For example, in the 1980s researchers identified the amino acid taurine as an essential amino acid for cats, which means cats cannot produce taurine so they have to ingest it by eating animal tissue.

In 1988, Paul Pion, D.V.M., a resident veterinary cardiologist at the University of California at Davis (UC Davis) found that commercial cat foods did not contain sufficient amounts of taurine. The processing of commercial pet food basically inactivates taurine levels in commercial foods. During that time, one of the leading causes of death in cats was dilated cardiomyopathy, a weakening of the heart muscle. Pion observed considerable improvement among cats with cardiomyopathy when their diet was supplemented with taurine.[1] In response to Pion's findings, pet food companies began adding supplemental taurine to cat foods. Subsequently, cases of cardiomyopathy dropped.

The research is still ongoing for identifying other essential amino acids for cats—which ones cats can produce on their own, and which ones they must get through food. "To date, the essential amino acids cats must obtain from the food they eat are arginine, histidine, isoleucine, leucine, lysine, methionine, phenylalanine, threonine, tryptophan, valine, and taurine," according to veterinary researchers Rory Foster, D.V.M., and Marty Smith, D.V.M.[2] While the research is ongoing, what is certain is that protein from meat contains a far greater variety of amino acids than do proteins from plants.

Vegetarian Cats?

Over the years I have received a number of letters from people inquiring about vegetarian or vegan diets for cats. The pet owners are vegetarian or vegan, so in turn they are interested in their animal companions also eating this way. In brief, I do not recommend this kind of diet for cats. In addition to the fatty acids and amino acids already mentioned, felines require a number of nutrients, and some can only be obtained from animal sources.

For instance, Vitamin A for vision, immune function, and fetal development can only be obtained from meat sources with liver being the richest source. Vitamin B12, required for enzyme function, is present only in animal products. Cats cannot synthesize niacin from sources such as dairy products and eggs. Cats obtain niacin from meat, which is a rich source of vitamin A. Pet food manufacturers add synthetic vitamin A to commercial cat foods and this vitamin can be added to vegetarian diets, however, it is not something I would do.

Supplementing taurine is possible, but I have learned that the main source for taurine supplements (and most other added vitamins and supplements) comes from China. There are companies that sell supplements for cats that can be added to a vegan diet, but you must take great care to be sure your cat's vegetarian diet is adequate in other areas. A representative from the Vegetarian Society of the United Kingdom states, "Cats fed on vegetarian diets are likely to look elsewhere for their preferred meat diet, and my cats will hunt and kill small rodents and birds."[3]

Carbohydrates

A cat's diet must also contain other sources of energy, in particular carbohydrates and fats. Carbohydrates usually come from plant sources such as cereal grains, seeds, and vegetables. In the wild, cats consume very few carbohydrates other than what they ingest from the intestinal contents of their prey. This usually amounts to less than 5% of their diet.[4] In contrast, most commercial cat foods contain between 30% and 70% carbohydrates. Why? "Carbohydrates are cheaper and more readily available as an energy source than proteins," according to veterinary researchers Foster and Smith.[5]

The problem with large amounts of carbohydrates in commercial pet foods is that they may be responsible for a number of health problems in cats. It is well established that obesity and maldigestion can occur in cats fed dry foods containing high levels of carbohydrates. "Obesity occurs when an animal's energy needs are exceeded and the extra glucose created by the digestion of the carbohydrates is stored as fat," according to veterinarians Foster and Smith.[6] Symptoms of maldigestion can include excessive gas and diarrhea.

Some pets also develop allergies to certain grains used in dry cat foods. Allergies can affect the skin and digestive system. Alfred Plechner, D.V.M., was among the first to identify food allergies as a source of illness in cats and dogs. In his book, *Pets at Risk: From Allergies to Cancer, Remedies for an Unsuspected Epidemic*, Plechner writes, "Today's cats, like dogs, are developing surface signs of allergies at a younger age. Typical indicators are persistent biting, licking or scratching of the skin; inflamed skin, lumps, bumps, or recurring sores; and inflamed ears with repeated infection."[7] Plechner suggests changing the sources of both carbohydrates and protein in the diet: for instance, switching from potatoes to rice, rice to barley (or other high quality grains such as quinoa) every four to six months. (See Chapter Twelve, Recipes for Cats.)

Two of the top-rated grains for overall highest percentage of daily values for protein, fiber, riboflavin, vitamin B-6, zinc, copper, and iron are two "pseudo grains," amaranth and quinoa (pronounced *keen-wah*). Interestingly, both amaranth and quinoa are ancient grains revered by the Aztecs and other ancient civilizations thousands of years ago. Only recently have these grains gained in popularity among North Americans for their own food and for making pet food. These high quality grains can be found in most natural foods stores. Several natural pet food companies I mention in Chapter Ten use these grains in some of their products.

Quinoa is not a true cereal grain, but rather the botanical fruit of an herb plant, very high in protein and calcium. Grains such as barley, corn, and rice generally have less than half the protein of quinoa.[8] Humans consider quinoa to be almost "perfect" because it contains all eight essential amino acids needed for tissue development in humans. The quinoa seed is also high in iron, vitamin E, and several B vitamins, and is gluten-free.[9]

Amaranth is not a true cereal grain, but is actually referred to as an herb or even a vegetable, although you cook the amaranth seeds like a grain. Amaranth has great nutritional value; it is high in protein, and high in the amino acid lysine, which is usually low in cereal grains. Just 150 grams of amaranth supplies 100% of an adult human's daily protein requirement. Amaranth is also high in fiber, low in saturated fats, gluten-free, and rich in vitamins and minerals. Recent studies have linked amaranth to reduction in cholesterol.[10] So, consider using amaranth or quinoa as a grain source, among others, when cooking for your animal companions—and for yourself!

Fats for Cats

Healthy fats are a highly efficient source of energy and are necessary for the absorption of some vitamins, including vitamins A, D, E, and K. According to T.J. Dunn, D.V.M., "Fatty acids (there are over 70) are important for a wide array of cell structure components and for many chemical reactions in the body, including hormonal and energy activities."[11]

Cats require both linoleic and arachidonic fatty acids in their diet. Linoleic fatty acid is present in poultry fat, sunflower oil, safflower oil, corn oil, flaxseed oil, and evening primrose oil. There are lower levels in olive oil. Arachidonic fatty acid cannot be made within a cat's body, so it must be consumed. Arachidonic fatty acid is found only in some fish oil and animal tissue, therefore, cats must consume meat as a source for this essential fatty acid.

If the diet is deficient in fatty acids it can lead to dry fur, scaly skin, and impaired wound healing. According to the Vegetarian Society of the United Kingdom, "Meat is the only major source. Arachidonic acid deficiency takes some time to develop but its effect on the cat is profound."[12]

Fiber is the insoluble carbohydrates that resist digestion in the small intestines. Fiber is found in plants and grains, and provides a number of vitamins and minerals as well as improves colon health. Some grain sources with high levels of fiber that you can add to your cat's diet are amaranth, barley, bulgur, oat bran, oat groats, and rye flake. Canned pumpkin, which many cats love, is also a good source of fiber. My twenty-year-old cat, Simon, suffers from occasional constipation and I simply add about ½ teaspoon of bran to his diet for a couple of days. It has worked very well for him for many years. Lynn Friday, D.V.M., recommends adding baby food green beans to a homemade diet for a constipated cat.

Keep in mind that the fiber used by most commercial pet food companies is inferior, and it is usually listed on pet food labels as beet pulp, peanut hulls, pectin, and corn by-products. Also, the percentage of carbohydrates in commercial foods—a common source for fiber—is far greater than what cats need.

Vitamins and Minerals

In all the years I have prepared a homemade diet I have never supplemented the food. I have found that if I feed my cat or dog a balanced diet, supplementation has not been necessary. In some cases, supplementing the diet can do more harm than good. Vitamin A is a good example. Excesses of this fat-soluble vitamin are stored in the liver and can lead to hepatic damage. In addition, cats cannot synthesize some vitamins from precursors (pre-vitamin structures) in the diet. Vitamin A can be divided into two categories; one a vegetable source (beta-carotene) and the other an animal source (retinyl palmitate). According to one of the top pet-health web sites, ProVet Healthcare, "Cats and mink are two species that are obligatory carnivores and they cannot use carotene, so they need to have vitamin A from animal sources. This is one of the reasons cats cannot be fed a vegetarian diet."[13]

Excess vitamin D, another fat-soluble vitamin, can also cause problems. Too much vitamin D can cause soft tissue calcification, general weakness, and poor motor reflexes. If you think your cat needs additional supplements, be sure to consult with an animal nutritionist or a veterinarian who understands, in-depth, cats' nutritional needs.

Malabsorption

In some cats and dogs, malabsorption can be a major problem. This means you may be feeding your cat healthy foods, but he or she is not absorbing nutrients from the food. Alfred J. Plechner, D.V.M., has looked at this problem extensively in his more than forty years as a veterinarian. "Malabsorption is a major problem that veterinarians do not discuss much," noted Plechner. "I find that about 70 percent of my patients cannot digest food properly. The problem is frequently due to the endocrine-immune defect that causes a destabilization of IgA [immunoglobulin A] in the gut, leading to subsequent inflammation in the intestinal lining."

Plechner also notes, "Often a lack of adequate digestive enzymes can be the culprit, and specifically a deficiency of trypsin. Trypsin is a major pancreatic digestive enzyme that contributes to the breakdown of protein, fats, and carbohydrates. The classic sign of a deficiency is animals eating their own stool....When animals cannot extract enough nutrition from food, they will often turn to stool eating." Basically, this means cats eat their own stools, or dogs eat the cat's stool because there is so much undigested protein still available.

Oftentimes, the solution for the enzyme problem can be fairly simple. The addition of a quality, pet-digestive enzyme supplement mixed directly into the food, may take care of malabsorption. "The supplements provide missing enzymes that help break down food and help the absorption of essential nutrients," according to Plechner, who recommends pet digestive supplements derived from plant sources. He advises to never use "supplements made from bovine or porcine sources because pets may be intolerant to beef and pork." In addition, plant-based enzymes are less expensive.[14]

Problems with Salmon and Tuna Diets

Even though it is generally understood that too much fish is not healthy for a cat, pet owners still consider fish a highly desirable treat for their cats, and do not see any harm in an occasional fish dinner. In turn, cats seem to relish fish or tuna juice. This conception gets reinforced by the pet food industry, which offers a variety of foods that include fish. However, the studies and research I found on this topic confirm that *fish is not, nor has it ever been, a natural diet for cats*, and can actually have adverse affects on cats' health if consumed regularly.

Fish is a rich source of protein and essential fatty acids, but fish can also cause a number of problems for cats. In a paper published by veterinarians at the University of California, Davis (UC Davis), they noted, "Clinical signs of vitamin K deficiency have been observed in cats offered two commercial canned diets high in salmon and tuna."[15] In the same study, they noted that coagulation times returned to normal after vitamin K therapy. The best-known function of vitamin K is its role in the blood clotting mechanism. Vitamin K deficiencies include increased blood coagulation times and generalized hemorrhage, resulting in death in some cases.

The relationship of a tuna diet and health problems in cats was also noted in a research paper by veterinarians at the Department of Physiology, Cornell University. "When observed in their home cages, cats fed commercial, tuna fish cat foods were less active, vocalized less, and spent more time on the floor and more time eating than cats fed commercial beef diets."[16] Cats in this same study also had "elevated tissue levels of mercury and selenium." The elevated levels of mercury and selenium were found in the tuna the cats ate.

In 1966, authors Kristine Nowell and Peter Jackson conducted an extensive survey on wild cats, looking at the ancestors of the domesticated cat and what their diets included. Their conclusion: "We came to the realization that only one of its members—the jungle cat—includes fish in its diet, although it still hunts predominately rodent prey."[17]

Some cats actually become addicted to a fish diet and refuse to eat any other foods. Without a doubt, the fish smell is very appetizing for cats, but this can be a dangerous and life-threatening diet. One cat owner shared her harrowing story of her cat eating tuna fish. She titled her blog, "Never Feed Cats Tuna Out of a Can."

> About two years ago, I thought that I would give my cat a treat she would love, so I bought Chicken of the Sea tuna fish in the can. After a couple of weeks I noticed she would hide under the furniture. I thought that was odd, but I ignored it and continued feeding her tuna fish. Shortly after that I noticed that she seemed to have trouble keeping her tongue in her mouth. I picked her up and noticed the fur had come off her neck and the skin was raw where she had been scratching it.

> I took her to the vet. He asked me, "What are you feeding her?" I told him, "Tuna fish from the can." He said that she was allergic to it and her throat was swollen and closing up inside. He felt her stomach and told me that her liver was swollen. He said if I had continued giving her tuna, it would have caused liver failure. She was put on an antibiotic and she pulled through it.

> The vet told me that it is not healthy to give cats tuna from the can. Now I do not buy my cat any cat food that contains tuna. Hope this helps someone.

Hopefully, this will inspire you to get fish out of your cat's life! A good way to wean your cat off an all-fish diet is to add the new food gradually, mixing it in with the fishy favorite. In time, you should be able to eliminate the fish diet completely.

Hyperthyroidism

Hyperthyroidism is caused by an increase in the production of hormones from the thyroid glands, which are situated in the neck.

Symptoms include weight loss even though the cat has increased its food intake. Affected cats often drink a lot of water and urinate excessively. There may be periodic vomiting or diarrhea, and the cat's coat may look unkempt. Hyperthyroidism was first recognized in 1979 and there has been a marked increase in the rate of diagnosis of feline hyperthyroidism since then. However, it is unclear if the increased incidence of hyperthyroidism is actually due to an increase in the disease or increased awareness.

There are some interesting studies that draw a correlation between an increase in the disease and commercial pet food. Veterinarians at UC Davis undertook a case-control study to search for potential risk factors for this disease. Owners of 379 hyperthyroid and 351 control cats were questioned about their cats' exposure to potential risk factors, including breed, demographics, medical history, indoor environment, chemicals applied to the cat and environment, and diet. The study found that two genetically-related cat breeds, Siamese and Himalayan, had a diminished risk of developing hyperthyroidism. No details were given as to why these two particular breeds were less likely to develop the disease.[18]

The researchers in this same study also noted, "Compared with cats that did not eat canned food, those that ate commercially prepared canned food had an approximate 2-fold increase in risk of disease." In addition, "The results of this study indicate that further research into dietary and other potentially important environmental factors are warranted."[19]

In a similar study conducted at Purdue University in 2004, veterinarians questioned if feline hyperthyroidism was the result of the aging of the cat population—cats living longer—and whether consumption of canned foods at various times throughout a cat's life could be associated with an increased risk of hyperthyroidism. The Purdue study looked at the medical records of 169,576 cats, including 3,570 cats with hyperthyroidism. The cats were evaluated at nine veterinary school hospitals during a twenty-year period. They also investigated 109 cats with hyperthyroidism (cases) and 173 cats without hyperthyroidism (controls). The results of this study showed that hyperthyroidism increased significantly from 1978 to 1997.

The report noted: "Overall, consumption of pop-top canned vs. dry food at various times throughout life and each additional year of age were associated with greater risk of developing hyperthyroidism. In female cats, increased risk was associated with consumption of food packaged in pop-top cans or in combinations of pop-top and non-pop cans. In male cats, increased risk was associated with consumption of food packaged in pop-top cans and the age."[20] This study suggests that not only aging in cats but also eating canned cat foods may play a role in hyperthyroidism.

Dry Cat Foods and Potential Problems

Dry cat foods are generally top-heavy with carbohydrates, and depending on the quality of cat food you buy, these ingredients can carry little if any nutritional value. Remember, cats need high protein diets, so if you are only feeding your cat dry food, you can likely expect health problems sooner rather than later. Excessive carbohydrates are not healthy for cats and can lead to obesity and allergies.

When purchasing a dry food for your feline, read the label and check to see what is in the product. Based on what you now know about the inferior ingredients used by most pet food companies, choose a dry food carefully, if at all. Be sure the overall protein content is *at least* between 18% and 27%. Remember, stay away from meat by-products, since that source of protein is highly questionable. (See Chapter Two.) Make sure meat, in one form or another, is listed as the first, second, and even third ingredient. Pet food companies will often list a meat source first on the label followed by grains as the second, third, and fourth ingredients. Beware! When you put the grain sources together you will most likely find that the grain ingredients far outweigh the meat ingredients in the food.

Another reason to avoid feeding dry, commercial cat food is its tendency to constipate cats. They need water in their food, which is available in canned foods.

There is also the option to bake cat crunchies from scratch, using human-grade food. That way, you know exactly what is in the food. (See Chapter Twelve for cat crunchy recipes.) Your cat will thank you for this!

So, if you think you are doing your cat a favor by just feeding a dry diet, think again. From a common sense perspective, could *you* be healthy and happy on a dry-food diet your entire life?

Baby Food for Sick Cats

When a cat is not well and refuses to eat, often times all-meat baby food will start him or her on the road to recovery. Sometimes veterinarians will recommend baby food for short-term use because the food is smelly, plus it is easy for a cat to digest.

I have often fed baby food to my cats when they were sick, and it helped. Usually, I would only feed them baby food for a few days before getting them back to their normal diet. Avoid all baby foods that contain onion powder because onions can cause health problems for cats—specifically anemia. Both onions and garlic contain an alkaloid disulfide compound, which is toxic to both cats and dogs. Cats ingesting onions have been shown to develop a condition called "Heinz body," where inclusions (denatured hemoglobin) attach to the red blood cells, and this leads to anemia.

My Final Word on Cats

I have always shared my home with both cats and dogs. I can honestly say I do not prefer one over the other—they both make wonderful companions and for very different reasons. Many people find that having two cats is a great option because they play together, sleep together, eat together, and become fast friends, especially if you get them as kittens. I have always gotten kittens in pairs, yet there are a couple of times a cat has come into my life as a stray. In that situation, I usually got another cat to keep him or her company. All of my cats have been indoor cats, which adds to their longevity. One cat, two cats, or more, they are great companions and bring much joy to my life. That is why it's easy for me to take the time to prepare home-cooked meals. I want them to live long, happy lives.

In 2005, my male Siamese, Yakkie, died at the age of twenty-seven. In 2008, my three-quarter Siamese, Simon, turned twenty-one years old and acts like a much younger cat. Many people have written to tell me how well their cats and dogs are doing on a homemade diet. Cooking takes more time than opening a can or bag, but at least you know what you are feeding your cats. In the long run, you will have a happier and healthier companion.

12

Recipes for Cats

A cat's diet is different than a dog's diet. Cats require meat as a source of protein where as dogs can obtain protein from grain sources. Meat contains an essential amino acid, taurine, that cats must have. If taurine is missing from a cat's diet, this can cause blindness and cardiomyopathy, a disease of the heart muscle. Most dry commercial cat food is made strictly from grains and includes a synthetic form of taurine, added to the mix. This is a huge reason why you should never feed your cat a strictly dry commercial food. (See Chapter Eleven for more information on this.)

The diet I cook for my felines is comprised of two-thirds meat as a protein source, which I regularly rotate among chicken, turkey, lamb, or beef. Cats like small chunks or slices of meat they can chew on, so I do not purée the meat.

The other one-third of my cats' diet is comprised of grains, and vegetables and/or fruit. A food processor is a great help when making food for both cats and dogs. Running cooked grains through a food processor increases digestibility and palatability for your cat.

Vegetables and fruits should also be put through a food processor or blender and puréed to a mush so your cats can digest them properly. If you only cut the vegetables and fruit into chunks or slices, most of this food will go through your cat undigested with few nutrients absorbed. If your cat is finicky, he or she may not even eat chunks of veggies or fruits.

In general, cats choose one or two diets they like and they tend to ignore other foods you may offer them.

When you give your cat a new food start by adding a small amount to their current diet. Increase the amount of the new food gradually. The following recipes are simple and nutritious, and a great way to begin cooking for your felines. Keep in mind that you can substitute grains according to what your cat likes. The recipes are categorized as follows:

- Tasty Meals for Healthy Cats
- Special Diets for Cats with Health Concerns
- Kitten Food

TASTY MEALS FOR HEALTHY CATS

Chicken, Rice, and Vegetables
2 cups of ground or chopped chicken, cooked
1 cup of cooked brown rice
¼ cup grated carrots

Cut chicken into small pieces. Run carrots and rice through a food processor. Mix chicken and carrots with rice. (You can also substitute rice with gluten-free quinoa or amaranth, or use another high quality grain.) If there is any fat from the chicken, pour about two teaspoons over the mix. Serve at room temperature.

SOURCE: ANN N. MARTIN

Fancy Sole Dinner

½ lb. fillet of sole
2 tbsp. parsley, chopped
1 tbsp. butter
1 tbsp. flour
½ cup milk

¼ tbsp. cheddar cheese, grated
2 tbsp. liver
¼ tsp. iodized salt
⅔ cup cooked noodles (can
    substitute cooked rice or grain)

Put sole in a small, greased baking dish. Sprinkle with parsley. Add enough water to cover the bottom of the dish. Cook in a preheated 450° F. oven for 10 minutes. Remove from oven and cool. Cut into kitty bite-size pieces.

Melt butter in small saucepan. Stir in flour and heat until bubbling. Gradually stir in milk and cook, stirring constantly until mixture thickens. Add cheese, liver, and salt. Stir until cheese has melted. Do not boil.

Cut up cooked noodles into kitty bite-size pieces. Add chopped fish and noodles to cheese sauce and stir. Cool and serve.

Source: Tony Lawson
The Cat-Lover's Cookbook

Quick Feline Eggfest

This one is about as simple as they come and it is a natural food for cats or other small predators. This diet is high in protein, vitamin A, iron, and B vitamins.

2 eggs
⅓ tsp. bone meal (or 250 mg. calcium or 1/8 tsp. eggshell powder)
¾ tsp. nutritional yeast

Use a fork to mix the yolks and whites together a bit, stirring in the bone meal. (Bone meal can be purchased at a health food store.) Sprinkle the yeast on top and serve raw. If you are not using organic eggs, you may want to cook them lightly to guard against salmonella.

This provides one meal or about half a day's rations for a ten-pound cat (or small dog). A small cat might eat just one egg per meal.

Source: Happy Babbish, D.V.M.

Finicky Feline Diet

1 cup chopped cooked chicken
¼ cup cooked rice
¼ cup chopped broccoli and carrots cooked until tender
Chicken broth

Mix all ingredients in a food processor or blender with enough chicken broth to hold together. Store in an airtight container in the refrigerator.

SOURCE: ANN N. MARTIN

Spot's Stew

This recipe is based on Spot's Stew canned food, made by Halo, Purely for Pets. A good choice for cats and kittens. The company was generous to share this recipe for one of its basic, quality cat foods. (See Chapter Ten for more on this pet food company.)

1 whole chicken
16 oz. brown rice
7 or 8 carrots
6 or 7 stalks of celery

2 or 3 yellow squash
2 or 3 zucchinis
1 small crown of broccoli
A handful of green beans

Rinse off chicken thoroughly and place in a large stew pot. Cover with water. Cut all veggies into small pieces, and add to the stew pot along with the rice. Cover and cook for 1 ½ to 2 hours, depending on the size of the chicken. Once the chicken is well-cooked, debone. Pour veggies, rice, broth, and chicken into the blender and purée into kitty bite-size pieces.

This food can be put in sealable plastic bags and frozen. Remove and thaw as needed. Some cats, particularly older ones, like this food puréed to a mushy consistency. Others prefer more chunks in the food.

Salmon and Rice Diet

5 oz. salmon, canned with bones
½ large egg, hard boiled
⅓ cup rice, long-grain, cooked

1 calcium carbonate tablet
  (400 mg. calcium)
1 multiple vitamin-mineral tablet

Mix together and serve. **Note:** This should not be a regular meal since too much fish is not healthy for cats. Once in awhile this makes a great treat. (See Chapter Eleven on fish diets for cats.)

SOURCE: DONALD R. STROMBECK, D.V.M., PH.D.
Home Prepared Dog and Cat Diets

Liver Feast

2 cups chopped beef or
  chicken liver
2 tbsp. vegetable oil

1 cup cooked oatmeal
¼ cup frozen peas, steamed

Cook liver in vegetable oil and chop finely or run through the processor. Add cooked oatmeal and peas. Cool and serve at room temperature.

Leftovers for a Feline Smorgasbord

If you eat healthy meals, natural non-processed foods, then your cat can share in the leftovers. Remember, no spicy or heavily seasoned meats or foods. No delicatessen meats.

1½ cups leftover meat (Beef,
  chicken, turkey or lamb are okay,
  but do not add pork because it is
  too rich and may cause diarrhea.)

½ cup leftover veggies, carrots,
  zucchini, sweet potato, squash, or
  sprouts
¾ cup mashed potatoes, rice, or
  oatmeal
1 tbsp. vegetable oil

Run veggies and rice or any grain through a food processor. Chop meat finely. Add meat to veggies and potatoes, rice, or oatmeal. Stir in a healthy oil such as flaxseed oil, olive oil, or a high-grade vegetable oil. Serve.

SOURCE: ANN N. MARTIN

Liver and Kidney Dinner

1 cup cooked or ground liver or kidney
¾ cup cooked oatmeal

3 tbsp. grated carrots or zucchini
⅓ cup plain yogurt
3 tsp. butter

Mix ground meat, oatmeal, and vegetables together. Melt butter and pour over mixture. Stir in yogurt. Serve at room temperature.

Salmon Feast

Fish is an excellent source of protein but as mentioned in the previous chapter, fish should not be fed on a daily basis. It is best to avoid feeding tuna, but a salmon treat once in awhile is tasty and healthy.

One 15 oz. can of salmon
1 cup cooked brown rice

¼ cup chopped parsley or celery
3 tbsp. plain yogurt

Drain salmon. Mix in brown rice, vegetables, and yogurt. Serve at room temperature.

Ann's cat, Simon, after a home-cooked meal.
PHOTO: ANN MARTIN

Raw and Organic Food

The less you cook the ingredients, the more nutritious it will be for your cat. Organic ingredients highly recommended, especially with the meat, to cut down on risk of salmonella.

3 cups organic ground meat (beef, chicken, turkey, or lamb). Raw or lightly cooked.

1 cup raw or slightly cooked organic organ meat (kidney, liver, heart, lung)

1 cup well-cooked grain (oats, rice, barley, cornmeal or quinoa)

½ cup vegetables (zucchini, carrots, squash or green beans)

1 tsp. olive oil or flax seed oil

I always use raw vegetables put through the processor to maximize on nutrients. However, some cats will not eat raw vegetables of any kind, but will eat them if they are cooked.

Mix all ingredients together, and then divide into individual portions. If you freeze the individual portions, they will keep for several weeks and you can defrost one-a-day. When thawing, try not to use the microwave or another cooking method, since this will reduce nutrient levels. Instead, let food thaw overnight in the refrigerator.

To warm it, place the food in a plastic bag with zipper closure, then immerse the bag into hot (not boiling) water for 10 minutes. Be sure to wash your hands thoroughly when handling raw meat.

The amount of food prepared with this recipe should last for about 5 days for an adult cat of normal size, 7 to 12 pounds. Your cat may eat more or less at each meal; use common sense to decide on serving size. Because this mixture is slightly lower in calories than dry cat food, you will need to serve slightly more of it in comparison.

SPECIAL DIETS FOR CATS WITH HEALTH CONCERNS

Senior Cat's Diet

1 cup boiled chicken
¼ cup broccoli, steamed

¼ cup shredded carrots, steamed
Chicken broth, approximately ½ cup

Mix ingredients with enough chicken broth to hold it together. All ingredients can be run through a processor, making it easier for an older cat to eat.

SOURCE: ANN N. MARTIN

Grain-Free Diet for Cats

Some cats, because of allergies or other health problems, may not tolerate grains in their diet. This diet provides an excellent alternative. You may also try "pseudo grains" quinoa or amaranth, which are gluten-free and high in protein and calcium.

1 lb. ground turkey, chicken, or beef
⅓ cup grated carrots
⅓ cup broccoli chopped in blender
¼ cup liver puréed in blender

4 to 8 vitamin tablets, powdered. (These can be purchased through your veterinarian or pet supply store.)

Mix together, put in freezer bags, and thaw as needed.

SOURCE: HEALTHY RECIPES FOR PETS[1]

Special Diet for Cats with Diabetes or Kidney Problems

Diabetics need fiber, and cats with kidney failure problems need to limit their protein intake, so this diet serves two purposes.

1 egg
1 tbsp. minced, cooked green beans
1 tsp. shredded carrot (If you substitute other vegetables, avoid the ones with a lot of natural sugars such as sweet potatoes, yams, and peas.)
2 tbsp. baked chicken breast minced (no skin)

⅓ cup cooked brown rice (Quinoa is a good alternative, high in calcium and protein, and gluten-free)
1 tsp. olive oil (Good for preventing hair balls and constipation, a common problem for diabetics)

Mix all the ingredients together thoroughly with a wooden spoon or in a blender/food processor. It is important to get the rice mixed in well so your finicky cat can't pick out the rice.

Cook in a small skillet over low heat, stirring and "chopping" constantly, until the egg is at least soft-set but done. Refrigerate in air-tight containers. This would make one or two meals for your feline.

Use within 36 hours (refrigerated). Stores well in the freezer in Zip-Lock baggies and can be thawed and warmed simultaneously in boiling water in the bag.

Source: Healthy Recipes For Cats[2]

Restricted Mineral and Sodium Diet for Felines

¼ lb. liver (beef, chicken or turkey only)
1 lb. ground beef, cooked
1 cup cooked white rice without salt

1 tsp. vegetable oil
1 tsp. calcium carbonate (health food stores or ground egg shells)
1/8 tsp. potassium chloride (salt substitute products)

Add a balanced supplement, which fulfills the feline minimum daily requirement for all vitamins and minerals, and add 250 mg. taurine per day.

Cook the meat. Stir in remaining ingredients, and mix well. Keep extra food covered in refrigerator.

Yields 1 ¾ lbs. of food.

Low-Fat Diet

4 oz. lean ground beef
½ cup cottage cheese
2 cups cooked carrots
2 cups cooked green beans

1 tsp. bone meal (available from a health food store)
½ tsp. catnip

Cook beef and drain fat. Mix with other ingredients. Sprinkle with catnip. This diet will feed a 15-pound cat for 3 days.

SOURCE: EDMUND DOROSZ, D.V.M.

Restricted Protein Diet for Felines

¼ lb. liver (beef, chicken or turkey)
2 cups cooked white rice without salt
2 large hard-cooked eggs, finely chopped
1 tbsp. vegetable oil
1 tsp. (5 grams) calcium carbonate (health food stores or ground egg shells)
1/8 tsp. potassium chloride (salt substitute products)

Add a balanced supplement, which fulfills the feline minimum daily requirements (MDR) for all vitamins and minerals, and add 250 mg. taurine per day.

Dice and braise the meat, retaining the fat. Combine all ingredients and mix well. Add water (not milk) as necessary to increase palatability. Keep extra food covered in refrigerator.

Yields 1 ¼ lbs. of pet food.

Allergy Diet

2 cups ground lamb
½ cup grated carrots or zucchini
1 cup brown rice
¼ cup cottage cheese

Combine all ingredients and either mix in blender or serve as is at room temperature.

Get Well Feast

(Easy on the stomach)

1 cup of leftover beef (cooked)
¼ cup alfalfa or parsley
½ cup cooked cream of wheat
¼ cup creamed cottage cheese

Blend and process ingredients into a thin consistency. Serve warm.

Feline Hypoallergenic Diet

Cats are developing surface signs of allergies at younger ages. Typical indicators are persistent biting, licking or scratching skin; inflamed skin, lumps, bumps, or recurring sores; and inflamed ears with repeated infection.[3]

Begin with a protein that your cat has never eaten before such as duck, venison or rabbit. Check with a local butcher shop, these meats are usually available or can be ordered. If your cat is allergic to chicken, there is a good chance he or she will be allergic to other types of fowl.

⅔ of the ingredients should be meat
⅓ white potatoes

As a source of fiber, I suggest adding a little finely grated zucchini, which is unlikely to cause an allergic reaction.

SOURCE: ALFRED PLECHNER, D.V.M.
Pets at Risk

The Add-Back Plan for Food Allergies

If you have trouble figuring out what your cat might be allergic to, Dr. Plechner's "Add Back Plan" is a good way to figure this out. Start with a restricted diet of just two ingredients; one of them a meat for protein. For instance, try chicken and cottage cheese, or chicken and zucchini. Cottage cheese works fine for most animals. Watch your cat's stools during this time: they should be well formed with no sign of mucous or blood.

If there are no signs of continued allergic reactions for one week, such as itching or diarrhea, then slowly add back ingredients, one at a time, in small amounts initially. Allow seven days for each add back ingredient to watch your cat's reaction. As you begin to add back, use home-cooked ingredients, organic if possible. Try starting with chicken and simple vegetables.[4]

If you identify two or three proteins that work, use one for two or three months, then rotate to a different protein. Do this with the grain as well, if possible. This will cut down on future allergic reactions to these foods.

SOURCE: ALFRED PLECHNER, D.V.M.
Pets at Risk

Especially for Kittens

Newborn Kitten Diet

1 12. oz. can of whole evaporated milk (or goat's milk)
A couple tbsp. plain yogurt (not nonfat)

If you have to feed newborn kittens, mix undiluted, canned evaporated milk with a few tablespoons of plain yogurt. This mixture can be refrigerated and warmed in a pan or hot water. If you use a microwave, use medium heat and check carefully to be sure it's not too hot. Feed as needed. Goat's milk is an excellent substitute.

Kitten Supplement

A recipe that is often used by breeders for orphaned kittens.

12 oz. of water
1 envelope of Knox Gelatin
1 12 oz. can of whole evaporated

milk (not skim)
2 tbsp. mayonnaise
2 tbsp. plain yogurt (not nonfat)

Boil the water, add the gelatin, and stir well. Add the following ingredients in order, mixing well after each addition.

½ of the canned milk (6 oz.)
2 tbsp. of mayonnaise

2 tbsp. of yogurt
Add the rest of the milk.

You could also include a kitten vitamin and/or pureed baby food meat, lamb, chicken, or beef.

Kitten Breakfast

1 tbsp. nonfat dry milk   3 tbsp. cottage cheese
3 medium eggs   2 tbsp. grated veggies or sprouts

Mix the milk powder with a little water, add eggs, and mix together. Cook. Once the mixture is cooked, turn it over, and put the cottage cheese and veggies or sprouts on top. When this is firm, fold it over like an omelet. Cut into bite-size pieces for your kitties.

Kitty Cookies

1 cup whole wheat flour   ¼ cup soy flour. (If your cat is
1 tsp. catnip   allergic to soy, you can use rice
⅓ cup milk   or rye flour.)
⅓ cup powdered milk   1 egg
2 tbsp. butter or vegetable oil   2 tbsp. wheat germ
                                 1 tbsp. unsulfured molasses

Preheat oven to 350° F. Mix dry ingredients together. Add molasses, egg, oil, and milk. Roll out flat on an oiled cookie sheet and cut into small, bite-sized pieces for a kitten.

Bake for 20 minutes and let cool. Store the cookies in a sealed container.

SOURCE: HEALTHY RECIPES FOR PETS[5]

Kitty's Favorite Treats

1 ½ cups cooked chicken or turkey   1 cup cornmeal
1 large egg   ½ cup whole wheat flour
2 tbsp. chicken broth

In a blender or processor, whirl chicken, egg, and broth until smooth. Scrape into bowl. Add cornmeal and ½ cup flour, stir until moistened. Cover dough and refrigerate at least 2 hours.

Roll out ¼ inch thickness on lightly floured board. Cut into ½" squares or triangles. Scatter on greased, 12" x 15" baking sheets. Bake at 350° F. until golden (about 15 minutes).

Remove from oven, let cool. Refrigerate in airtight containers for up to 2 weeks. Freeze for longer storage.

SOURCE: NoCans.com[6]

Audrey Hepburn anticipates a new home.
PHOTO: SUMNER FOWLER

13
Cooking for Dogs

Many people have told me that they are terrified about feeding their dogs anything other than what comes out of a can or bag labeled "pet food." They worry they may be harming their animal companions by feeding them home-cooked meals or table scraps. A couple of pet owners have even admitted they believe their pets will keel over and die if fed a homemade diet.

Sadly, this fear reflects very effective marketing by commercial pet food manufacturers who portray themselves as the true authorities on what constitutes "a balanced and nutritional" meal for your dog or cat. If you review Chapter Two, and the ingredients that can legally be mixed into commercial pet food, I hope you will be convinced to try cooking for your dog. At the very least, try to incorporate fresh healthy food along with a high-quality pet food.

I have been cooking for my dogs and cats for nearly nineteen years and not one of my animal companions has died because of food-related problems. In fact, they have lived far longer than the expected life spans and I believe this is largely due to eating healthy, home-cooked food. My large dogs lived almost twice as long as predicted for large-breed dogs, and my cats lived more than twenty years on average. One of my dogs, Sarge, a German Shepherd, had been diagnosed with discoid lupus, and even *he* lived two years longer than the veterinarian had predicted.

Most veterinarians receive *minimal* education for dog and cat nutrition while in veterinary school, and generally are not well informed on good nutrition for pets. However, there are some veterinarians who specialize in holistic or naturopathic veterinary medicine and they understand good nutrition. If you are worried about cooking for your animal companions, find a veterinarian who specializes in nutrition. If your animal companion has a serious health problem, then first consult a holistic or naturopathic veterinarian before you try to cook for your pet. These holistic veterinarians can guide you on preparing a home-made diet, and how often to feed your dog, especially if he or she has health problems.

A Balanced Diet

In order to maintain health, your dog needs a combination of protein, carbohydrates, fiber, and fats. Ultimately, there are a lot of unknowns regarding a "complete and balanced" diet for dogs and cats, although there are many who claim they have the answers. Martin Goldstein, D.V.M., writes in his book, *The Nature of Animal Healing*, "Our pets, like us, are all individuals, all with different requirements. So what works for one may not work for another."[1]

The following suggestions for home cooking for your dog are not based on scientific evidence, but rather accumulated knowledge and sound advice from veterinarians and nutritionists knowledgeable about balanced and complete meals for cats and dogs. If you talk to ten different experts on dog nutrition, you will get at least half a dozen different opinions, or more. Some add supplements, some don't; some advocate less protein for kidney problems, some don't; some say feed your dog twice a day, others may advise three meals a day.

After talking with numerous nutrition experts, I concluded that the best combination of ingredients for my dog's meals is one-third protein, one-third carbohydrates, and one-third vegetables and fruits. I then add small amounts of high-quality vegetable oil, which I discuss later in this chapter. If this combination I am suggesting does not work for your dog, then consult with a holistic veterinarian or pet nutritionist.

My dog and cats eat three meals a day: breakfast, lunch, and dinner. My dog, Kodi, is a one-hundred-sixty-pound Newfoundland and in addition to three meals a day, Kodi gets two snacks during the day. These snacks might include homegrown sprouts, or maybe a piece of cheese, carrot stick, apple slice, or a dog cookie that I've baked. Depending on the size of the dog, and his or her dietary requirements, many pet owners feed their dogs two meals per day, usually in the morning and in the evening. With the giant dog breeds, it is easier on their systems if they eat three or four smaller meals a day rather than one or two large ones. More frequent meals also help protect against bloat, which can be deadly. (See Chapter Fifteen on bloat.)

A Basic Diet for Dogs

My dog begins his day with a bowl of cooked oatmeal, about one-and-a-half cups, along with a small amount of meat or fruit mixed in. Lunch and dinner include meat, grains, and fruit or vegetables. (See Chapter Fourteen, Recipes for Dogs.) A basic home-cooked meal for your dog should include the following:

- **PROTEIN;** sources can be cooked meat (beef, chicken, turkey, lamb), fish, eggs, or dairy products. These protein sources provide many, if not all, of the amino acids your dog requires. The ancient "pseudo grain," quinoa, is an excellent source of protein. While most grains are deficient in the amino acid, lysine, quinoa has an adequate quantity of lysine, therefore, quinoa is considered to contain all the essential amino acids, making it a complete protein.[2]

  If you are thinking about feeding your pet pork, keep in mind that this is a rich meat and may cause diarrhea in some dogs and cats, so use cautiously. Also, if you serve pork, be sure it is well cooked. For some dogs, turkey in large quantities may also be too rich. Be sure to remove turkey and chicken skin, since these have a lot of animal fat.

  Keep in mind that some dogs are allergic to eggs. (Two of my dogs were allergic to eggs.) You will know if your dog is allergic if he or she vomits or gets diarrhea a short time after eating even a small amount of egg. (See the section later in this chapter on "Food Allergies.")

  Some people believe that feeding your dog raw meat is the best way to go. For me, I always cook my animal companions' meat. I have researched all aspects of the meat industry, including conditions at many slaughterhouses, and I have decided that I am not willing to risk my dog getting seriously ill from ingesting contaminated raw meat.

  I realize that cooking the meat destroys some of the healthy enzymes, but cooking also kills harmful bacteria and parasites. Based on the research I undertook regarding the controversy surrounding raw vs. cooked meat, I concluded that it is not safe to feed a raw diet to companion animals. In my second book, *Protect Your Pet: More Shocking Facts*, I have written about this extensively.

I do include a recipe for raw food in Chapter Fourteen for those who want to feed raw foods; however, I strongly encourage you to use organic meat, and veggies and fruit. Also, there is a good alternative if you want to feed your dog raw meat, veggies, and fruit without the risk of salmonella. The pet food company, The Honest Kitchen, makes raw, human-grade pet food that is dehydrated. The dehydration process kills potential parasites and harmful bacteria without destroying the nutritional value of raw foods. (See Chapter Ten.)

- **GRAINS OR CARBOHYDRATES**; options include brown rice, oatmeal, pasta, mashed potatoes, shredded wheat, whole grain cereals, and whole grain breads, plain or toasted. There is an array of grains to choose from—just be sure that they are well cooked for proper digestion.

   Carbohydrates also provide calories to maintain weight. Carbohydrates and fiber come primarily from grains and vegetables, and provide energy and stamina.

- **VEGETABLES AND FRUITS**; carrots, zucchini, summer squash, peas, yellow and green beans, yams or sweet potatoes, mushrooms, apples, pears, watermelon—just about any fruit—are good for dogs. (No grapes or raisins.) You can feed your dog vegetables raw or steamed. My dog eats his vegetables and fruit raw, but I know many people who lightly steam the vegetables. Be sure the veggies are finely chopped, sliced, or run through a food processor for increased digestibility.

   CAUTION: Cabbage, broccoli, and Brussels sprouts tend to cause gas, so only use small amounts. If fresh vegetables are not available, you can use frozen vegetables, which retain a much higher level of vitamins and minerals than do canned vegetables.

   If your are still wavering over whether or not to cook for your dog, remember this; sources of fiber that pet food manufacturers can legally use in commercial pet food include animal hair, peanut hulls, beet pulp, and even ground-up paper. Indigestible proteins, such as those used in many commercial pet foods—including feathers and fecal matter—obviously cannot sustain an animal.

   Contrast these sources of acceptable ingredients from the pet food industry with pets eating a home-cooked diet with human-grade ingredients.

- **Vegetable Oil;** add daily from one teaspoon (for small dogs) to one tablespoon (for large animals) of vegetable oil with essential fatty acids (EFAs). In *The Whole Pet Diet*, author Andi Brown notes, "The most important EFAs for your pet's optimal skin and coat health occur in pure edible vegetable oils, such as wheat germ, sunflower, safflower, and soy oils. These oils contain abundant amounts of critically important linoleic and linolenic acids."[3] She adds, "Some fish oils can be equally beneficial, and the fish flavor may help your pet adjust to this addition to its diet."

A natural vegetable oil provides your pet with added energy, a lush coat, clear skin, and good muscle tone. Flaxseed, olive, and sesame oil, although more expensive, are excellent if your pet has an immune deficiency. These oils should be refrigerated to prevent them from becoming rancid. Olive oil can be stored safely in a dark, cool cupboard, preferably in a dark-tinted glass bottle.

Supplements

Some veterinarians recommend adding supplements to a homemade diet, while others do not think it is necessary as long as the home-cooked meals are made from healthy unprocessed foods. In the nearly two decades I have been cooking for my dogs and cats, I have not needed to add supplements and my pets have done extremely well. However, my dog, Sarge, who had been diagnosed with discoid lupus, did take special supplements recommended by his holistic veterinarian to deal with his medical condition.

My dog enjoys a mid-day treat of bean sprouts, parsley, or alfalfa. These are sources of many minerals, vitamin C, and fiber. Your local health food store can usually provide a variety of seeds that you can grow in jars at home. It is easy to do, and you will have an abundance of sprouts in no time. If you have children, this is a fun family project, and a way to teach your children about good nutrition for dogs and humans! Mung beans are the most popular sprouts to grow, and lentils have an excellent mild flavor. Most sprouts will keep for seven to ten days in your refrigerator.

Food Allergies and Malabsorption

Food allergies can be a major problem for some dogs. Veterinarians Shawn Messonnier and Alfred Plechner have written extensively about food allergies. In his article, *Using Whole Foods Supplements to Treat a Common Skin Disorder in Dogs*, Messonnier recommends regular bathing, whole food supplements, and proper diet. He writes that for those who don't have time to cook for their pets, natural brands are much better than the grocery store brands. He notes, "Most holistic doctors agree that a homemade diet, made with fresh organic ingredients, is best for the pets."[4]

In his most recent book, *Pets at Risk*, Plechner discusses malabsorption in dogs, which may require a quality, pet-digestive enzyme supplement. These supplements provide missing enzymes that help break down food and help the absorption of essential nutrients. Plechner recommends pet digestive supplements derived from plant sources, and these can be purchased over-the-counter.

Another possible reason for malabsorption, according to Plechner, is what he describes as "imbalances in the endocrine-immune system." He describes this condition at length in his book. (See Chapter Eleven for more information on malabsorption.)

If you are feeding your dog a nutritious, human-grade diet, and your dog still seems to be having health problems, you may want to learn more about malabsorption, potential food allergies, and endocrine-immune imbalances. In Chapter Fourteen, there is an "Add Back Plan" that will help you identify foods your dog may be allergic to.[5]

Calcium for Dogs

Your dog needs calcium in his or her diet. There are many natural food sources for obtaining this calcium. How much calcium do our pets need per day? In *Natural Remedies for Dogs* and *Natural Remedies for Cats*, Nancy Scanlan, D.V.M., suggests: "The recommended dosage for toy dogs is 100 mg. daily; small dogs, 200 mg.; medium dogs, 300 mg.; larger dogs, 500 mg. Large puppies can use 10 percent more."[6] Scanlan notes that dairy products provide calcium that is readily absorbed by both dogs and cats. However, calcium from cow's milk is not readily absorbed since it usually causes diarrhea in dogs. Scanlan warns that if you are feeding a 100% commercial diet, then do not supplement with calcium at all. "If you do, it can cause kidney stones," explains Scanlan.

In his book, *How to Have a Healthier Dog*, Wendell Belfield, D.V.M., advises, "It's too much, not too little that bothers me most in regard to calcium. Dog owners have this great urge to over-supplement calcium.

A balanced vitamin and mineral supplement should contain all the extra calcium a growing dog or pregnant or lactating bitch needs."[7] Individual animals have individual needs. If you are going to supplement your dog's diet, do so under the guidance of an animal nutritionist or veterinarian who understands supplements.

I add yogurt or cottage cheese to my dog's lunch or dinner meal for calcium. Yogurt is easily digested by pets and will replace the good bacteria in their systems if they are on antibiotics. Cottage cheese is another good source of calcium. Sabine Contreras, a canine nutritionist in Santa Monica, writes, "Cottage cheese is an excellent source of calcium, phosphorus, protein and vitamins; yogurt is a good source of calcium, protein, potassium and magnesium and (if products with live cultures are fed) can supply beneficial bacteria, for example Lactobacillus acidophilus."[8]

Low-fat milk provides a good source of calcium. However, keep in mind that some dogs (and cats) can be lactose intolerant. There are also good nondairy sources of calcium, such as the grain quinoa or canned salmon. The following are natural sources of calcium and their approximate doses of calcium per serving:

- Plain, nonfat yogurt contains 450 mg. of calcium per cup.
- Canned sardines with bones, about 3 ½ oz., provides 400 mg. of calcium.
- One cup of low-fat cow's milk provides about 300 mg. of calcium.
- Cottage cheese contains 155 mg. per cup.
- Quinoa is a gluten-free grain that is high in calcium. One cup of quinoa contains as much calcium as an entire quart of dairy milk.
- Canned salmon with bones, about 3 oz., contain 180 mg. of calcium.

Many vegetables contain calcium, although in much smaller amounts. The following are some of the common raw vegetables your dog would probably find interesting. The calcium content is based on one cup of the vegetable listed.

- Parsley contains 83 mg. of calcium.
- Celery has about 50 mg. of calcium.
- Green and yellow beans contain 41 mg. of calcium.
- Green peas have 36 mg. of calcium.
- Carrots have 34 mg. of calcium.
- Broccoli florets have about 34 mg. of calcium. (Use sparingly. This vegetable produces gastric gas.)

Crushed eggshells from free-range chickens are also a good source of calcium. According to Ken W. Koelkebeck, D.V.M., University of Illinois, "The egg shell consists of about 94% to 97% calcium carbonate."[9] Eggshells should be washed in hot, soapy water before crushing to prevent salmonella or bacteria contamination. Make sure the eggshells are finely crushed because large pieces might cut a dog's mouth. A small coffee grinder is perfect for crushing eggshells.

Vegetarian Dogs?

Controversy exists over the classification of dogs as carnivores or omnivores. Some sources unequivocally state that dogs are carnivores, while others maintain dogs do not have to eat meat to be healthy. Dogs *can* subsist on plant protein if fed a vegetarian diet. However, recent nutritional studies are finding that taurine from meat is necessary for a dog's cardiovascular health, especially in large and giant dog breeds.

In 2003, researchers at UC Davis published updated information on their findings in dogs who experienced dilated cardiomyopathy (DCM). They found a direct relationship between DCM and a lack of taurine in the diet. This was identified particularly in large-breed dogs. In their research at UC Davis, veterinary nutritionists Andrea Fascetti, D.V.M., and her colleagues, Quinton Rogers, D.V.M., and Robert Backus, D.V.M., documented low plasma taurine concentrations in dogs with clinical signs of DCM. Backus found "diet-associated taurine deficiency and cardiac insufficiency in more than half of a group of 21 privately owned Newfoundland dogs, which excreted extraordinary amounts of taurine in their urine."[10]

Another breed susceptible to DCM is the Doberman Pinscher. Studies on other breeds are underway to investigate possible causes for taurine deficiency. Hopefully, these studies will determine the quantities of dietary taurine needed to prevent DCM. A number of the pet food companies are now adding taurine to their lines of dry dog food.

Bottom-line, recent research shows that vegetable protein does not contain all the amino acids that dogs require. So if you plan on feeding your dog a vegetarian diet, be sure you get the correct formulation of ingredients to provide a balanced diet, and a source of taurine. The Vegetarian Society of the U.K. provides diets for both dogs and pups. These diets were provided by owners of vegetarian dogs living in Great Britain who found their dogs had "liked and thrived on the feeding regime."[11]

Should You Give Your Dog a Bone?

Pet owners often ask about bones as a good source of calcium for dogs. There are disadvantages in using bones as a source of calcium in home-cooked diets. Richard Pitcairn, D.V.M., author of *Natural Health for Dogs and Cats*, expresses his concerns over the high lead and other heavy metal content in bones, raw or cooked. "This is why it is important that the bone meal source has been checked for these substances," according to Pitcairn. "It is often bone meal from other countries, less industrial, that can be used while bones from cattle in the U.S. are often quite contaminated. This is one reason that you will find warnings on bone meal in garden supply centers, that it is not to be used in food. It is a little-known fact that commercial pet foods use bones from U.S. cattle and are often unacceptably high in lead."[12]

Pitcairn also points out that the phosphorus in the bone meal makes the requirement for calcium even higher. This would not be a problem in the natural state, but when we are feeding grains and vegetables, the balance of these minerals has to be adjusted accordingly. Pitcairn suggests, "A vegetable source of calcium therefore has the advantage of providing just calcium without the unwanted phosphorus."[13]

In addition to Pitcairn's concern about the calcium-phosphorous ratio in bones, there are real concerns about the danger of dogs eating bones—cooked or raw. Splintered bones can cause major digestive tract problems for dogs, so I do not recommend giving dogs bones—cooked or uncooked. Chewing on bones can also cause broken teeth, molar crown fractures, and endodontic (pulp) disease.

I have asked numerous veterinarians their opinion on dogs eating bones and there is general agreement that eating bones in any form is downright dangerous. The major problems with dogs eating animal bones are explained at length in my book, *Protect Your Pet: More Shocking Facts*.

—

The following chapter provides some simple, healthy recipes for your dogs. Generally, dogs love just about anything you prepare for them—and if they don't, you'll know quickly. Those particular ingredients the dogs don't like will still be in the bowl—or on the floor—after they've eaten what they like. A friend's dogs are incredibly talented at picking lettuce leaves out of the bowl and dropping them on the floor, while eating heartily the rest of their home-cooked meal.

The extra hour or two you spend once a week preparing a home-cooked meal will be one more way you can express your love and gratitude for one of your very best friends—or in many cases, your four-legged family members!

Sally, a shelter dog, longs for wide-open
areas with a companion.
PHOTO: SUMNER FOWLER

14

Recipes for Dogs

*O*ver the years, I have acquired a number of recipes for dogs, and have enjoyed cooking for my canine companions since 1991. I hope you can find a couple recipes to get you started on cooking for your dog. Remember, dogs are like people, they enjoy food variety, so have fun experimenting. I am sure your dog will appreciate your efforts.

Most of these recipes are made in bulk or for one or two dogs. Use as little or as much as your dog requires, depending on his or her size. If possible, buy organic meats, since even human-grade meats sold in the typical grocery store are usually pumped up with hormones and antibiotics. In addition, if you buy meat from a natural food store, it is likely that the farm animals were raised on a sustainable farm, not a factory farm, and were treated humanely until slaughtered. (If you want to learn more about human meat production and the problems with factory farming in terms of animal welfare, health, and environment, read Dr. Michael Fox's book, *Eating with Conscience: The Bioethics of Food.*)

Be creative when cooking for your companion animals. Just be sure your dog gets a recommended balance of protein, carbohydrates, and fats. Once a week I prepare a week's supply of home-cooked meals for my 160-pound Newfoundland. It takes no more than two hours to prepare a week's supply of food, which I freeze in individual containers and thaw as required.

Just before serving I add about a tablespoon of plain yogurt (a good source of calcium) and about a tablespoon of sunflower oil to my dog's food.

Some people are concerned that their pets are not getting all the vitamins and minerals they require when eating a homemade diet. If you worry about this, add a quality vitamin/mineral supplement. Personally, I don't supplement my dog's food since he is eating nutritious and balanced meals.

Foods to Absolutely Avoid

There are some foods that you should not feed your dogs. These foods can cause serious illness and even death. I have listed these foods in alphabetical order for quick reference. Foods to stay away from include the following:

Avocados: If a dog ingests this fruit it can result in difficult breathing and fluid accumulation in the chest, abdomen, and heart. Avocado leaves, fruit, seeds, and bark contain a toxic principle known as Persin.

Caffeine: Coffee, coffee grounds, tea, tea bags, and chocolate—all sources of caffeine—may cause big problems in dogs. Read the following description on problems with chocolate.

Chocolate: Theobromine, a substance found in chocolate and cocoa, is poisonous to animals. The darker the chocolate the more dangerous, with Baker's chocolate being the most harmful. For dogs, eating chocolate can result in seizures, coma, and death. If you have children, be extra careful their holiday candy and chocolates are not within reach of the dogs.

Grapes and Raisins: From April 2003 to April 2004 the Animal Poison Control Center (APCC) investigated 140 cases involving one or more dogs that ingested varying amounts of raisins or grapes. Of these, fifty animals developed clinical signs ranging from vomiting to life-threatening kidney failure. Seven dogs died. Exactly why grapes and raisins affect dogs to this extent is still uncertain, but this is a warning to owners not to feed either grapes or raisins to your dog. Also, be sure you do not leave grapes or raisins where your dog can get to them.

Garlic: Do not add garlic to your dog's diet thinking this will keep fleas away. Garlic is part of the onion family along with leeks and shallots. Research has shown that onions can be harmful, if not deadly, to our pets. Onions, garlic, chives, and other species of the plant genus Allium can be potentially toxic to pets. According to the National

Animal Poison Control Center (NAPCC), "Allium species contain sulfur compounds known as disulfides, which if ingested in large quantities can cause gastrointestinal irritation and could even result in damage to red blood cells."[1] The NAPCC advises pet owners not to feed any plants in the Allium family.

Macadamia Nuts and Walnuts: Although there have been few cases reported on the toxic affects of dogs ingesting these nuts, it would be wise to avoid feeding them. From 1987 to 2001 the Animal Poison Control Center (APCC) received forty-eight calls about dogs who had ingested these nuts. Their clinical signs included weakness, depression, vomiting, and tremor.

Pits and Seeds from Apples, Cherries and Peaches: Dogs love fruit—at least my dogs do—but the seeds and pits from fruits contain cyanide, which is poisonous. This applies to humans as well as dogs.

Xylitol: This is a sugar substitute found in chewing gum, baked goods, and toothpastes. It has been shown to cause liver failure in some dogs.

The following recipes are easy and highly nutritious. Plus, you know exactly what your dog is eating! It should not take you more than two hours to cook enough meals to satisfy your dog for a week. You can also prepare individual meals, every day, if you have the time. If you have a food processor or blender, this makes food preparation even easier, and the food more digestible for your dog. The recipes for dogs have been broken into the following categories:

- Wholesome Recipes
- Special Diet Considerations
- Vegetarian Diet
- Crunchies & Treats
- Puppy Food

WHOLESOME RECIPES

Chow Chow Chicken

2 chicken thighs or white meat
1 celery stalk, finely chopped
3 carrots, finely chopped

2 small potatoes, peeled and cubed
2 cups of rice, uncooked

Place chicken pieces in large pot. Cover with cold water. Add carrots, celery, and potatoes to water. Cover and simmer on low heat for about 2 hours until the chicken becomes tender. Add the rice. Cover and cook over low heat for about 30 minutes until the rice is tender and most of the liquid is absorbed. Remove from heat. Pull the chicken meat off the bone and discard bones and skin. Return shredded pieces to pot and stir well. Let cool. Store in refrigerator or freeze.

SOURCE: DEBORAH SMITH
Pet Owner

Sweet Potato Fritters

2 eggs
½ cup nonfat milk
2 tbsp. whole-wheat flour
2 tbsp. wheat germ

2 cups raw sweet potatoes, finely
  grated
1 tbsp. olive oil

Beat eggs. Add milk. Mix in flour and wheat germ. Fold in grated sweet potatoes. Fry over medium heat until cooked thoroughly.

SOURCE: KATIE MERWICK
People Food for Dogs

Dinner for Kodi

This is a recipe I make often for my Newfoundland, Kodi.

2 lbs. ground chicken or turkey, lightly cooked
2 cups couscous soaked in boiling water (or other favorite grain)
4 medium potatoes, cooked and mashed
3 carrots
2 apples, washed
1 zucchini
1 cup parsley

Put the carrots, apples, zucchini and parsley through the food processor and mix with remaining ingredients. This can be put in individual containers and frozen.

SOURCE: ANN N. MARTIN

Lunchtime Salad Treat

½ cup chopped wild shrimp, deboned organic chicken or wild crabmeat, cooked and cooled
½ cup mixed salad greens
1 tbsp. chopped alfalfa or red clover sprouts
1 tsp. olive oil
1 tbsp. cottage cheese or plain yogurt

In small bowl, toss and combine the shrimp, salad greens, sprouts, and olive oil. Transfer to serving dishes and top with the cottage cheese before serving. Freeze any portion you will not use within 2 or 3 days.

SOURCE: ANDI BROWN
The Whole Pet Diet

Macaroni, Liver, and Veggie Dinner

2 cups of elbow macaroni, cooked
2 pieces of beef liver cooked in
  butter or oil

About 12 oz. of mixed frozen
  vegetables, drained
1 cup of cottage cheese

Chop liver slices in pieces. Add macaroni and vegetables. Fold in cottage cheese. Serve.

Weimaraner Walleye Recipe

3 pounds walleye pike fillets
2 oz. chicken livers, diced finely
2 cups fish stock
3 cups cooked brown rice (or
  another favorite grain)
¼ cup cooked wild rice

¼ cup kale, frozen
½ cup green beans, frozen
½ cup collard greens, frozen
½ cup corn, frozen
¼ cup potatoes, frozen
1 tbsp. cod liver oil

Preheat oven to 350° F. In a baking dish add walleye fillets and diced chicken livers. Pour in fish stock and cod liver oil. Add frozen veggies, and cover and bake for 20 to 30 minutes or until done. In a large bowl add cooked rice and the juices from the baking dish, along with the cooked veggies. Mix well. Chunk the walleye into a size your dog can easily chew. Mix well. Allow to cool, then serve. Freeze leftovers or keep refrigerated.[2]

Beef Stew

One 16 oz. can of low-sodium
   beef broth
2 tsp. chopped parsley
2 carrots, chopped
2 celery stalks, chopped

1 cup of peas
1 cup of steak cubes, cooked
2 tbsp. cold water
½ to 1 tsp. cornstarch

Bring broth to a boil. Add vegetables and beef. Simmer 20 minutes. Combine cold water and cornstarch. Stir into stew.

SOURCE: KATIE MERWICK
People Food for Dogs

Chinese Style Dinner

2 cups of cooked brown rice (or a favorite grain)
1 cup cooked ground chicken
1 cup grated carrots, zucchini, or celery

Mix together, add 1 tbsp. vegetable oil, and top with alfalfa sprouts.

Ralph resides at a humane society, hopeful.

PHOTO: SUMNER FOWLER

151

Muttloaf

½ cup amaranth (See *Note)
1 ½ cups chicken broth
1 ½ lbs. ground chicken or turkey
½ cup cottage cheese
2 whole eggs

½ cup oats, rolled (raw)
¼ cup spinach -- finely chopped
¼ cup zucchini -- finely chopped
1 tbsp olive oil

Add amaranth and chicken broth to sauce pan and bring to a boil. Reduce heat and simmer for 20 minutes. Set aside and let cool. Preheat oven to 350º F.

In a large mixing bowl add meat, cottage cheese, veggies, and eggs. Mix thoroughly. Add wheat germ, cooled amaranth, and olive oil. Mix well. Add mixture to loaf pan, bake at 350º F. for 1 hour or until done. Note: Amaranth is an excellent grain that can be found in natural food stores. If not, use barley. Barley requires 4 cups of broth and 50 minutes to cook.

Canine Meat and Grain Bulk Menu

12 cups cooked brown rice (or another grain choice)
2 cups fatty meat (regular ground hamburger, fatty beef heart, beef chuck roast)

2 cups lean meat (chicken hearts, ground turkey, beef and chicken liver, whole chicken or turkey, lean beef heart)
1 ½ cups grated or chopped vegetables

Mix all ingredients together; or steam meat and vegetables, and then add rice. Serve the daily ration slightly warm.

SOURCE: RICHARD PITCAIRN, D.V.M., PH.D.
Natural Health for Dogs and Cats

Spaghetti with Meat Sauce

8 oz. whole-wheat spaghetti,
    cooked and drained
1 lb. hamburger, fried

4 medium mushrooms, cut in
    pieces
1 medium tomato, chopped
½ cup tomato juice

Mix hamburger with mushrooms, celery, and chopped tomato Stir in tomato juice. Pour over spaghetti and serve warm.

Veggie Pot Pie

FOR THE PIE CRUST:

2 ¼ cups flour
⅓ cup cold water

¼ cup vegetable oil
¼ tsp. salt

PIE INGREDIENTS:

2 cans cream of potato condensed
    soup
1 cup of milk

¼ tsp. thyme leaves crushed
¼ tsp. pepper
4 cups cooked cut vegetables

Preheat oven to 400° F. Combine crust ingredients. Separate into two balls. Roll into two 9" x 13" crusts. Lay one crust on bottom of greased 9" x 13" baking dish.

Mix other ingredients in bowl. Spread vegetable mixture evenly on top of crust. Lay second crust on top of vegetable mixture. Bake 30 minutes or until crust is golden. Let stand 10 minutes before serving.[3]

A Leftover Feast

4 cups leftover roast beef, chicken, turkey or fish.

2 cups leftover mashed potatoes, sweet potatoes, or yams.

1 cup finely grated carrots, zucchini, celery, or any other non-gas-producing vegetable that is in the refrigerator.

Mix all together and top with 2 tbsp. of plain yogurt and 1 tbsp. sunflower oil or olive oil.

When I am traveling I often make leftover meals (leftovers from human meals), put them in freezer bags, and freeze them so Kodi will have some of his favorite leftovers while we are away. He will know that Mom is thinking of him.

SPECIAL DIET CONSIDERATIONS

Pensioner's Birthday Party Casserole

(for the older pet)

1 cup cooked turkey or chicken

2 tbsp. bacon fat or vegetable oil

8 lasagna noodles

1 egg

1 tbsp. wheat germ oil

1 tsp. bone meal

Cook noodles as directed on package. Drain. Line bottom of 8" x 8" pan. In medium-sized bowl, mix chopped turkey or chicken with bacon fat, egg, wheat germ oil, and bone meal. Spoon over noodles and spread. Cover with layer of noodles. Bake 30 minutes in 350° F. oven. Let stand for 15 minutes before cutting.

SOURCE: EDMUND R. DOROSZ, BSA, D.V.M.
Let's Cook for Our Dogs

Weight Reduction Diet for Adult Dogs

½ lb. chicken, cook

2 cups rice, long-grain, cook

¼ tsp. salt substitute (potassium chloride)

A dash of table salt

4 bone meal tablets

1 multiple vitamin-mineral tablet

Mix all ingredients. Feed portions according to your dog's size.

SOURCE: DONALD R. STROMBECK, D.V.M.
Home Prepared Dog and Cat Diets

Venison and Potato Diet for Adult Dogs

4 ½ oz. venison (raw weight), cooked

3 cups potatoes boiled with skin

2 tsp. vegetable (canola) oil

$^1/_{10}$ teaspoon table salt

4 bonemeal tablets (10 grain or equivalent)

$^1/_5$ multiple vitamin-mineral tablet (made for adult humans)

Mix all ingredients. Feed portions according to your dog's size.

SOURCE: DONALD R. STROMBECK, D.V.M.
Home Prepared Dog and Cat Diets

Canine Hypoallergenic Diet

Begin with a protein that your dog has never eaten before, such as duck, venison, or rabbit. If your dog is allergic to chicken, there is a good chance he or she will be allergic to other types of fowl.

½ protein

½ white potatoes

As a source of fiber, I suggest adding a little finely grated zucchini or summer squash, which is unlikely to cause an allergic reaction. The meat and potato mix should be about equal portions.

SOURCE: ALFRED PLECHNER, D.V.M.
Pets at Risk: From Allergies to Cancer, Remedies for an Unsuspected Epidemic

The Add-Back Plan for Food Allergies

If you have trouble figuring out what food your dog might be allergic to, Dr. Plechner's "Add Back Plan" is a good way to figure this out.

Start with a limited diet of one protein and one carbohydrate. Cottage cheese and white potatoes work fine for most animals. Watch your dog's stools during this time; the feces should be well formed with no sign of mucous or blood.

After seven days, if there are no signs of continued allergic reactions, such as itching or diarrhea, then slowly add back ingredients, one at a time, in very small amounts initially, allowing seven days for each ingredient. Watch your dog's reaction to each new ingredient. Use home-cooked ingredients, organic if possible. For starters, try adding back chicken, then a simple vegetable like summer squash or zucchini.

Once you identify two or three proteins and grains that work, then rotate these combinations every two or three months to avoid future food allergies. Be sure you avoid any "treats" that are not part of your add-back plan; these could throw off identifying correctly allergic reactions to foods.[4]

SOURCE: ALFRED PLECHNER, D.V.M.
Pets at Risk: From Allergies to Cancer, Remedies for an Unsuspected Epidemic

Convalescing Diet

If your dog has undergone surgery or is recovering from an illness, this is easy on the stomach.

2 cups of cooked cream of wheat   I cup grated parsnips
1 soft boiled egg   1 tbsp. melted butter
1 ½ cups cottage cheese

Mix together and serve warm.

SOURCE: EDMUND R. DOROSZ, D.V.M., B.S.A.
Let's Cook for Our Dog

VEGETARIAN DIET

Easy Vegetarian Kibble for Dogs

4 cups of a 3-grain cereal   1 tbsp. kelp
2 cups rice flour   1 tsp. cod liver oil
½ cup whole wheat flour   ½ cup vegetable oil
1 tbsp. bone meal   400 I.U. vitamin E
1 tbsp. yeast (enriched, if possible)   4 eggs

Mix dry ingredients until combined, then add wet ingredients and stir until moist. Drop into ½ tsp. pieces onto greased cookie sheets and bake at 350° F. for 30 minutes. Remove from oven when lightly browned.[5]

CRUNCHIES & TREATS

Ann's Crunchies for Dogs and Cats

1 ½ cups whole-wheat flour
1 ½ cups rye flour
1 ½ cups brown rice flour
1 cup wheat germ

1 tsp. dried kelp or alfalfa
4 tbsp. vegetable oil
1 ¼ cups beef or chicken broth
   or stock

Mix dry ingredients. Slowly add broth and vegetable oil. Roll out into a thin sheet. Place on cookie sheet and bake at 350° F. until golden brown. Cool and break into bite-size pieces. Store in air-tight container in refrigerator.

SOURCE: ANN N. MARTIN

Chicken Crunchies

1 ½ lbs. chicken wings, necks, backs, and liver, cooked and ground.
   (These can be ground either with a conventional meat grinder or
   in a food processor. Some whole foods stores sell frozen, ground-up
   chicken necks.)
One 15 oz. can of salmon,
   mackerel, or tuna in oil
1 ½ cups rye flour
2 cups whole-wheat flour
2 ½ cups brown rice flour
1 ½ cups wheat germ

5 tbsp. vegetable oil
4 tbsp. powdered kelp
1 ½ cups powdered milk
¾ cup brewer's yeast
4 cups of beef or chicken stock

Mix dry ingredients. Mix in ground chicken and fish. Mix beef or chicken stock with vegetable oil. Blend into dry mix. Roll to ¼ inch thickness and place on cookie sheet. Bake at 350° F. until golden brown. Break into pieces. Store in air-tight container in refrigerator.

Peanut Treats

2 ¼ cups whole wheat flour
¾ cup all purpose flour
1 ¼ tbsp. baking powder

1 ¼ cups peanut butter
1 cup milk

Combine flour and baking powder in a large bowl. Combine milk and peanut butter in a separate bowl and mix until smooth. Gradually stir peanut butter mixture into flour in the larger bowl.

Knead dough by hand and roll out on floured surface to desired thickness. Cut out treats.

Place aluminum foil on cookie sheet and bake 15 minutes at 400° F. Cool before storing.

Note: Cooking time may vary depending upon thickness.[6]

Meat-Free Dog Biscuits

2 ½ cups flour
¾ cup powdered milk
½ cup vegetable oil
2 tbsp. brown sugar

¾ cup vegetable brother
½ cup carrots (optional)
1 egg

Preheat oven to 300° F. Mix all ingredients into a ball and roll out to about ¼ inch thickness. For fun, use cookie cutters, or cut into strips. Place on cookie sheet and bake for 30 minutes. This is a great recipe to do with young children learning to cook. They will be delighted when the dog gobbles up their treats![7]

Cheese and Bacon Biscuits

¾ cup wheat flour
½ tsp. baking soda
1 stick soft butter or margarine
⅔ cup brown sugar
1 egg
1 ½ tsp. vanilla

1 ½ cups uncooked oatmeal
1 cup shredded cheddar cheese
⅔ cup wheat germ crumbled (can
    substitute more oatmeal)
½ lb. bacon, cooked crisp

Mix the flour, butter, and sugar together in a bowl, adding one ingredient at a time until you have a good firm dough. Then drop the dough in clumps with a spoon onto an ungreased baking sheet. Bake at 350° F. for 15 minutes, then turn off the heat and let the biscuits cool for several hours until dry and hard. Best if stored for a few days at room temperature before using, and then refrigerate.[8]

Puppy Food

Mother's Milk Replacement for Puppy

1 cup (low- fat) cow or goat milk
1 egg yolk
2 drops infant vitamins (human)

1 tsp. corn oil
2 drops cod liver oil

Mix and refrigerate. Warm to body temperature before feeding. Feed as much as the puppies will eat or when their tummies are full and they are content.

Source: Edmund R. Dorosz, BSA, D.V.M.
Let's Cook for Our Dog

Puppy Meat Loaf

1 lb. ground beef
One 24 oz. container cottage
   cheese
4 eggs
½ cup dry milk powder

¼ cup wheat germ
8 slices oatmeal bread, crumbled
8 cups cooked oatmeal
4 cups cooked brown rice

In very large mixing bowl, combine ground beef and cottage cheese; blend well. Add eggs, milk powder, and wheat germ. Mix. Add the crumbled bread, oatmeal, and brown rice. Mix well.

Divide among ten small (about 5 ½" x 3-½") aluminum loaf pans. Place on a cookie sheet and bake at 350° F. for 1 hour. Cool at room temperature for 1 hour, then promptly refrigerate. This food is perishable, so don't store it in the fridge longer than three days.

We always freeze all but one of the loaves. To defrost a loaf, let it stand in the refrigerator overnight. Crumble the meat loaf into a bowl, drizzle with some water, and microwave for 20 to 30 seconds, until warm. Watch for hot spots after microwaving. Puppies will gobble this up!

Make sure to discard any food that has been sitting out for 30 minutes or longer.

SOURCE: PAT PETERSON
Breeder of German Shepherds

Pretzels For Your Pup

1 tsp. brown sugar
2 tsp. active dry yeast
⅔ of a cup water
¾ cup whole wheat flour
3 tbsp. soy flour, low fat
¼ cup nonfat dry milk
1 tbsp. dried liver powder

1 tbsp. bone meal flour
Pinch of salt
1 beaten egg (half in glaze, half in recipe)
2 tbsp. cooking oil
3 tbsp. wheat germ

Dissolve yeast and sugar in warm water. Combine dry ingredients. Add half of the beaten egg, oil, and yeast water mixture. Mix well. Knead on a well-floured board until dough is firm. Place in oiled bowl, cover, and let rise until double in bulk.

Shape the dough into pretzels and place on greased cookie sheet. Bake in preheated 375° F. oven for 15 minutes. Remove and brush with beaten egg and sprinkle with wheat germ. Return to oven and bake at 300° F. for about 15 minutes until nicely browned and quite firm.

NOTE: If you can't find bone meal flour and liver powder, you can omit them.[9]

15

Bloat: A Canine Killer

I have shared my home with dogs for many years, including two Saint Bernards, four Newfoundlands, and a German Shepherd. All of them were either giant-breed or large breed, and they were prone to bloat.

In the mid 1990s, a friend had a Great Dane who died one night after bloating. This immediately compelled me to begin learning more about this problem. I wanted to be sure this didn't happen to one of my big dogs, and I wanted to warn others with large-breeds. Fortunately, I have never lost a pet to bloat, but there are plenty of tragic stories of others who were not so fortunate. Hopefully, this information will help others keep their giant and large-breed dogs safe from bloat.

What Is Bloat?

Bloat is a condition that affects primarily large and giant breeds, the Great Dane being at the top of the list. Bloat is second to cancer as a primary cause of death in large dogs. Bloat, or gastric dilatation-volvulus (GDV), happens when there is a rapid build-up of air in the stomach. In a large percentage of bloat cases, torsion occurs when the stomach twists, for reasons yet unknown, cutting off the esophagus at one end and the small intestines at the other.

163

At first, a dog with bloat experiences shock because the distended stomach puts pressure on the large veins in the abdomen that carry blood back to the heart.[1] Without proper return of blood, the output of blood from the heart is diminished, and the dog's tissues are deprived of blood and oxygen.

In bloat cases, 25% occur when the stomach fills with gas and the increased pressure compresses both ends of the stomach, preventing the gas from escaping. In the other 75% of bloat cases, this condition is caused by the stomach actually twisting.

In recent years the number of bloat cases has increased dramatically, and studies are pointing to dry dog food as one of the culprits. Jerold Bell, D.V.M., from Tufts University, found that there has been a 1500% increase in the incidence of bloat in the past thirty years. He identifies several diet-related factors that are associated with a higher incidence of bloat. "These include feeding only dry food, or feeding a single large daily meal," reports Bell. "Dogs fed dry foods containing fat among the first four ingredients had a 170 percent higher risk for developing bloat."[2]

A bloat study undertaken by M. Raghaven, D.V.M., at Purdue University, showed, "Inclusion of table foods in the diet of large and giant breed dogs was associated with a 59% decreased risk of GDV [gastric dilatation-volvulus], while inclusion of canned foods was associated with a 28% decreased risk."[3]

Dogs at Risk for Bloat

Most notably, giant breeds and breeds that are described as "deep-chested" are at the greatest risk for bloat. Deep-chested dogs means the length of their chest from backbone to sternum is relatively long while the chest width from right to left is narrow. This physical characteristic and its connection to bloat applies to deep-chested purebred dogs as well as mixed breed dogs.

According to Bell, "Canine bloat, or gastric dilatation-volvulus (GDV), is the number-one cause of death for several large and giant breeds."[4] The giant breed with the highest average likelihood of a bloat episode is the Great Dane at 42.4%. Other large breeds affected by bloat include Akita, Great Dane, German Shepherd, St. Bernard, Irish Wolfhound, Bullmastiff, Great Pyrenees, Bernese Mountain Dog, and Irish Setter.

Dogs weighing more than 99 pounds have an approximate 20% risk of bloating.[5] The Irish Setter, Akita, Standard Poodle, German Shepherd, and

Boxer are at higher than average risk for getting bloat. Other large breeds that experience bloat, but have a lower incidence, include the Labrador Retriever, Golden Retriever, Old English Sheepdog, Weimaraner, Collie, Bouvier des Flanders, Samoyed, and Alaskan Malamute.

Even small dogs have experienced bloat, although it happens rarely. A few breeds that were mentioned in the research include the Miniature Poodle, Dachshund, and Pekinese.

Causes of Bloat

Veterinarian Lawrence Glickman, a noted authority on bloat, has identified a number of risk factors in GDV. In a five-year study of eleven giant and large breed dogs, Glickman and his team at Purdue University found that during the study, twenty-one dogs (2.4%) and twenty dogs (2.7%) of the large- and giant-breed dogs, respectively, had at least 1 episode of GDV per year of observation, and 29.6% of these dogs died. The findings of this study showed:

- As the dog aged there was a 20% increase in the risk of developing GDV per year.
- There was a 63% increase in the risk associated with having a first degree relative with GDV.
- The rates of GDV also increased if a dog tended to eat quickly or gulp food.[6]

Risk Factors Associated with Bloat

In addition to giant- and large-breed dogs eating primarily dry foods, Glickman identified some other risk factors that could be contributing to the increase in bloat in dogs. These risk factors could be corrected with minimum effort.

Raised Feeding Bowls: For many years, the consensus was that it was better to have raised bowls for feeding your dogs. Many pet owners, myself included, bought raised bowls for our giant breeds. The raised bowls were supposed to prevent dogs from gulping air when eating. Many manufacturers and pet suppliers were making claims that the raised bowls aided a dog's digestion and prevented bloat. Researchers are now finding that raised feeding bowls are a part of the problem.

In one of Glickman's studies on bloat he found that a raised feeding bowl actually increased the risk of bloat by 110%. The Glickman data showed that "approximately 20% and 50% of cases of GDV among the large and giant-breed dogs, respectively, were attributed to having a raised food bowl." Glickman concluded, "We have found no scientific research to support these claims "for the benefits of a raised bowl."[7]

Lean Dogs vs. Overweight Dogs: Another risk factor for bloat is that lean dogs are more predisposed to bloat than overweight dogs. According to researcher Bell, "It is hypothesized that this is because fat takes up space in the abdomen. The lack of fat in the abdomen of a lean dog creates a basic situation similar to that of a dog with a deep and narrow chest: A lean dog has much more room in the abdomen for the stomach to move around than a fat dog."[8]

Dr. Bell does not want to imply that overweight dogs are healthier, only that a dog's weight could be a factor contributing to bloat. In this situation, a dog that is too lean could be more inclined to bloat. On the other hand, overweight dogs are prone to diabetes, damage to joints, bones and ligaments, heart disease, reproductive problems, digestive disorders, increased risk of cancer and decreased quality and length of life. Excess weight can be detrimental, but a few additional pounds might be in order for a lean dog. Personally, I have always kept my dogs within five pounds, either way, of the recommended breed standard.

Emotional State of Dog: Glickman found that fearful, nervous, or aggressive dogs also have a much higher incidence of bloat than dogs who were perceived by their owners as having happy temperaments. Glickman also identifies stress as a factor in bloat. Causes of stress include the addition of a new pet to the family, a change in families, kenneling, even dog shows. In addition, Glickman noted that there is a slightly higher percentage of males than females who develop bloat.

Symptoms of Bloat

You know your dog best. If you recognize any change in his or her regular habits, then consider bloat as a possible reason for unusual behavior. Some symptoms your dog might experience if he or she has bloat include:

- Frequent attempts to vomit, usually unsuccessfully. This may occur every five to thirty minutes.
- Restlessness and anxiety
- Pacing
- Unproductive gagging
- Heavy salivating or drooling
- Abdominal swelling
- A hunched up appearance
- Persistent coughing

If your dog develops any symptoms of bloat do not hesitate to immediately take him or her to a veterinarian or to the nearest emergency clinic. A dog can die within an hour of experiencing these symptoms.

A Possible Genetic Connection

Glickman suggests not breeding a dog who has bloated since there might be genetic influences. He explains: "My own overview of what's happening and where I think all of this is leading in both this study and in other studies that, rather than a particular gene causing the condition, certain inherited characteristics predispose breeds or individual dogs to bloat."[9] Glickman recommends that you don't breed a dog if a first-degree relative has suffered an episode of bloat.

The owners of the kennel where we board our Newfoundland when we travel also own Mastiffs. During the 2006 winter holidays, one of their dogs bloated in the middle of the night. Fortunately, they were able to get to the emergency clinic and the dog survived. These pet owners had always been conscientious about bloat concerns in big dogs and had always followed the advice about avoiding bloat; fed smaller meals, curtailed exercise before and after meals, made sure their dogs ate slowly—but still, one of their dogs bloated. Later, they learned that the mother of this dog had died of bloat. Now they question if there is a genetic connection.

Prevention

There are no known ways to prevent bloat or predict if your dog will develop it. However, there are a few steps you can take that might be helpful in preventing bloat:

- Feed your dog two or three smaller meals during the day rather than one large meal.
- Make sure your dog avoids vigorous exercise for at least one hour before a meal and two hours after eating.
- Do not let your dog drink excess water after meals.
- Do not permit rapid eating. You might try putting another smaller dish in the middle of the bowl making the dog eat around it, which should slow down a rapid eating pattern.
- Feed your dog a high-quality diet. Inferior foods can cause gastrointestinal problems and excess gas.
- Do not elevate food bowls.
- When changing to a new dog food, do so gradually over a period of one or two weeks. Sudden diet changes can cause gastric problems.
- Avoid gas-producing products such as brewers' yeast, alfalfa, soybean products, peas, and beet pulp. Beet pulp is found in a number of pet foods as a source of fiber.
- If you are feeding your dog a dry food, avoid foods that contain citric acid. Citric acid in the stomach is conducive to forming gas.
- Always keep a product containing simethicone on hand to treat the symptoms of gas. Dog breeders recommend the antacids Gas-X, Phazyme, or Mylanta Gas, (not the regular Mylanta). If your dog shows signs of gas, burping, or flatulence, give him or her an antacid. If the other signs of bloat are present, do not hesitate to get immediate veterinary attention.

Planning Ahead

Always make sure you have your veterinary and emergency clinic's phone numbers next to your phone. Cases of bloat often occur in the middle of the night when your own veterinarian is not available. You want to have an emergency plan in place.

If you live alone and have one of the larger breeds, make arrangements with one or two of your neighbors who could help you get your dog into the car and to the clinic in an emergency.

If you have a dog who is at high risk for bloat and you live a distance from your vet or an emergency veterinary clinic, you might ask your vet to show you how to pass a stomach tube into your dog since this could save your dog's life. Keep in mind it usually takes two people to do this procedure, and it will only be effective if the dog's stomach has not already twisted.

Siefried Zahn, D.V.M., author of *Bloat in Large Dogs*, writes that a bloat first-aid kit should be available if you have breeds susceptible to bloat and due to distance, you might not be able to get your dog to a vet on time. These matters should be discussed with your veterinarian who can advise exactly how the procedure can be carried out. Zahn outlines the steps on the website, First Aid for Bloat. Visit: www.canadasguidetodogs. com/health/healtharticle6.htm

Veterinary Treatment of Bloat

If your dog bloats and you have to make a mad dash to the veterinarian, the vet will first administer fluids intravenously for treatment of shock. Next, pressure must be removed from the stomach and this may be done with a tube or insertion of a large needle through the skin and into the stomach. The stomach must than be returned to its proper position, which requires abdominal surgery. The surgical procedure is called "gastropexy," which permanently stabilizes the stomach by attaching it to a fixed structure in the abdominal cavity, such as ribs or the body wall. If this operation is not performed, bloat will likely occur again.

Gastropexy is a costly operation. In Canada and the United States, this procedure can cost between $2,000 and $3,000, but is well worth it because you will be giving your dog another chance at life.

16

Other Pet Concerns

*W*hile researching the pet food industry and pets in general, I constantly come across many other issues related to pets that ultimately affect their well-being. In this chapter, I discuss some of these issues. They stir up a combination of annoyance, grief, and disbelief with what some people will do for financial gain or convenience that ends up harming animals.

In some situations, such as the practice of declawing cats, I think there are pet owners who simply do not understand the profound negative impact on a cat. Hopefully, this chapter will be educational, and perhaps inspire readers to share this information with others.

Designer Dogs

Some people had e-mailed me about their concerns regarding "designer dogs" as the new hot item with hundreds of mixed breeds now on the market. Basically, breeders are playing with genetics, creating what they call "fun and interesting dogs" by crossbreeding unlikely matches. Ads in the paper and on the internet abound for "cock-a-poos," "peke-a-poos," "labradoodles," "goldendoodles"—the list is endless. Some of these designer pups are selling for exorbitant prices, $1,000 or more.

When I was a child, these mixed-breed dogs were called mutts, mongrels, or mixed breeds. Now they are classified as designer dogs. What is the difference between mutts and designer breeds? In mutts and mongrels, the parentage is unknown. In mixed-breed dogs, the breed of only one parent or grandparent is known.

With hybrids or designer dogs, the puppies are a result of mating two known breeds. For example, a Cocker Spaniel is mated to a Poodle and breeders call it a "cock-a-poo"; or a Labrador is bred to a Poodle to make a "labradoodle." I even found an ad for a "newfiepoo," which is a cross between a Newfoundland and Standard Poodle. Breeding these two types of dogs is a disaster waiting to happen. Both breeds are prone to hip dysplasia, bloat, and skin problems.

Alfred Plechner, D.V.M., writes about the tragedy of inbreeding and designer dogs in his book, *Pets at Risk*: "Although fashionable and beautiful on the surface, inside these animals are frequently damaged goods, suffering from physiological defects that render them unhealthy and less able to cope with life."[1]

The list of breeds being bred to Poodles includes a wide variety; Collie, Chihuahua, American Eskimo, Beagle, Bichon Frise, Brussels Griffon, Dachshund, German Shepherd, Jack Russell, Maltese, Schnauzer, Pomeranian, Pug, English Bulldog, Cairn Terrier, and even Saint Bernard. The theory behind breeding to Poodles is that Poodles do not shed or cause allergies. However, genetics does not necessarily offer up the same traits that humans plan on. Some dogs may fit the standards of a Poodle, others won't.

No breeder can guarantee the outcome of such breeding. Certain traits and characteristics of a breed can only be achieved by generations of breeding and eliminating the animals that don't have the desired traits until the right combination occurs. Breeders try not to breed dogs that have faulty physical characteristics. However, over-breeding can lead to the internal damaged goods that Plechner warns against.

For example, Standard Poodles often inherit Addison's disease, cataracts, progressive retinal atrophy, and skin problems. If bred to a Labrador Retriever, the health issues for the offspring could be considerable, including hip dysplasia, eye abnormalities, bloat, and cataracts, in addition to serious endocrine-immune problems.

Despite the fact that many breeders of designer dogs state that the dogs are purebred, that is not necessarily the case. Breeders are under the assumption that because the mother, perhaps a Poodle, and the father, a

Labrador, are purebred, the pups, "labradoodles," should also be classified as purebred. This is not the case because "labradoodles" and other designer dogs are not recognized as registered breeds. These dogs are simply a mixed breed that people have given an exotic name, along with a high price tag. Interestingly, there was an on-line survey showing photos of the designer breeds and mixed breeds from shelters. When asked to differentiate between the two, very few people could tell the difference.

I find it incredibly disheartening that some people are not willing to adopt a dog that is part Poodle and part Spaniel from the local shelter, but would pay lots of money for a puppy that has been labeled a "designer pup, cockapoo." This is a sad testimony to out-of-control consumerism and a disregard for the livelihoods of animal companions.

My advice: If you want a unique dog, visit your local shelter or pound. You will find a wide variety of dogs and pups all deserving good, loving homes. You will also be saving a life, saving a lot of money, and perhaps inheriting a wonderful companion with a personality that is unique, unforgettable, and life-changing for you.

Pet Scams on the Internet and in Newspapers

I spend a large part of my day on the internet, researching and communicating. One day I was on a list reading blogs from a number of people who had been scammed for hundreds and sometimes thousands of dollars. They were writing about individuals posing as pet owners who made passionate pleas for help to find their pets a better environment.

There are Internet ads and newspaper ads for English Bulldogs, Teacup Poodles, Malteses, Yorkies, Chihuahuas, and a number of other small-breed dogs. Photographs of cute puppies make the ad even more enticing, along with the low price, usually less than half the price for a purebred pup. Most ads also state that these pups are AKC registered and have had their first set of shots.

The ads appear in newspapers' classified sections throughout North America as well as in classified ads on the Internet. As soon as the media outlet is aware these ads are a scam, they pull the ad, but the scammers continue using different names and different cities and more ads. People who are aware that these ads are scams usually notify the paper or website owner and the ads are pulled quickly. I have done this numerous times. These scammers not only list pups but also kittens, monkeys, and rare birds.

As a regular visitor to a number of pet sites, I read quite a few letters from people who have been scammed. One young woman who got scammed wrote about her experience on an Internet blog:

> After e-mailing the owner of the Chihuahua that was for sale on the Internet, they told me that if I sent a $200 deposit they would go ahead and send me the puppy and I could send them the rest of the money. Well, getting all excited and telling my children, who are 3 and 5, we woke up early in the morning, and started out on a long trip to the airport, where the puppy was going to be shipped. The plane she was on was landing at 10:49 a.m. My children had drawn pictures for her, and were very excited.
>
> Well, after arriving there and sitting around for over 4 hours I was told that the puppy was not on the flight. I realized that this was a scam! The person will not reply to my emails. My children were so excited and now they are really upset.

Another woman who got scammed lost all of her Christmas money. She wrote:

> I went online to get my boyfriend a bulldog for Christmas. The ad said bulldog for sale for $90, so I replied. The person emailed me saying he still had the dog and that all I had to do was send him $90. Well I was so excited to get a dog for such a reasonable price that I went ahead and sent him the money, which was all I had for Christmas.
>
> After forwarding the $90, he sent me another email telling me that I had to send him the money for shipping. I told him that I didn't have it so he said that he would pay the shipping. Today he emailed telling me that he went to send her and he needs a new crate for her that would cost $250. I told him that I couldn't send that much. He told me to email the airlines, which I did, and they told me that a crate would be required to ship the dog. Now I'm waiting to hear back from this man about what else to he is going to do. I hope it's not a scam but I think its going to end up being one.

After hearing from a number of people who had got taken by these scams, I decided that perhaps the people perpetrating the scams might feel differently if the shoe was on the other foot. I replied to an ad from a scammer in Lycos, Nigeria who was selling English Bulldogs. This person claimed to be a Christian minister working in Lycos. He emailed me explaining he could not keep the pups because it was very hot in Lycos and he was afraid they would become ill. I let him go on for a while in email communications, telling me about the pup and how I should forward the money by Western Union. He told me I would be able to pick up the pup at the closest airport near my home in Canada.

Finally, after three or four days of back and forth e-mails, I advised him that I knew it was a scam. Then I told him I had forwarded the information to the authorities in Lycos and they would take appropriate action unless he refunded within two hours the money he had taken from all these people. He responded in a panic, claiming, "I told you that you were the first person I tried to scam. I have never taken money from anybody. I am just a poor boy still dependent for his parents. Imagine how my old mother will feel when I'm arrested." He went on at great length claiming his innocence.

I e-mailed him back and told him he did not seem to care when he took money from poor innocent people. In the following days, he sent two more emails begging my forgiveness and claiming he was a "young innocent boy trying to make his way through school." He said he had contacted his pastor and prayed to God for forgiveness. At one point, he even threatened suicide if I contacted the authorities. Sadly, you can bet he is right back doing the same thing again, and more people are being taken.

Never, *ever* send money to anyone by Western Union or Money Gram. Once you send the money, you have no way of tracing it nor any way to recover the money if the deal falls through.

"Puppy at the Airport" Scam

In this scam someone posts an ad on a pet Internet site or in a newspaper stating that there is a pup at the airport who has not been claimed. The airport is usually in Cameroon, Nigeria, but can be in other Nigerian cities. Of course, you have no way of knowing this until you reply to their ad.

The ad states that if no one claims this pup within three days, the animal will be put down. The email scam asks the reader to send three or four hundred dollars for shipping costs, a crate, vaccinations, and all the paperwork. The scammer assures you the pup will be sent to the airport closest to you and that you have saved the life of a pup. The money for all the pup's necessities is to be sent by Western Union. If you send the money, the scam is completed, and you never hear from the person again.

"Lost Dog Found" Scam

When a pet is lost, the first thing owners will do is search the neighborhood. Next, they will place an ad in the local newspaper or on a local Internet site. The scam around this scenario is the pet owner will receive a call from someone claiming to have picked up the dog, but the dog was injured.

People who run this scam claim to be truck drivers, salesmen, or movers, and their story is that they took the dog to a veterinarian in a town they were passing through. The town could be several hundred miles away or even in another state. They ask that you send them the money for the veterinary bills and on their way back they will return your pet to you. Like all other pet scams, they want the money wired to them. Don't do it. These people have no idea where your pet might be. Call the police and report the scam.

Another lost pet scam involves a caller who claims he has found a dog who might be the one you lost. The caller asks for a description of the lost dog and he then advises you that the one he found does not fit that description. It is a set-up.

A short time later, you receive another call from a person who tells you that she has found your pet and gives you the description of the dog she found. It matches the description of your dog and you get excited. Then the caller asks you to send the reward money and your pet will be returned. Do not fall for this one either.

One such incident occurred in March 2005 when a gentleman in South Carolina lost his dog, Lucky. He posted an ad on the Internet and soon heard from a man who claimed he had found the dog, but he was a distance away and it would cost $400 to ship the dog back home. The pet owner sent the money via Western Union, but the dog never arrived. Fortunately, the dog was found and returned by someone else shortly after this pet owner lost his money. Eventually, the scammer was arrested and charged with racketeering. He had scammed at least seventeen other pet owners in several states. This person had also run the scam asking people to send money for veterinary bills for their injured dog that he had found.

On the other hand, if you are the one who has found a pet, be very careful that you are returning the dog or cat to the rightful owner. Ask for photographs if necessary. Scammers will often claim a pet and sell it to a research facility.

Pet scams abound. If you are taken in by one of these scams, notify the authorities immediately. Perhaps you can prevent scammers from fooling someone else. Never, under any circumstances, send money to anyone by Western Union because the funds cannot be traced.

Boarding Your Pet

Thousands of pets spend time at boarding kennels each year. My concern is how many people really take the time to find out about the daily operation and services these facilities provide. I have heard horror stories from pet owners who left their companion animals at kennels that claimed to offer the best care, but in fact neglected, and even abused, some pets.

To locate a reliable and caring kennel in your area, start by asking your veterinarian or a friend for a recommendation. If you have to turn to the Yellow Pages of your phone book, be sure to do a background check on the kennel you choose. Check with the local Better Business Bureau to see if any complaints have been lodged against the kennel.

Next, call the kennel and make an appointment to visit the facilities. If you are planning to board your pet in the near future, ask if they have space available and if they can accommodate special needs your pet might have, such as medications, extra exercise for a young dog, or extra care for an elderly pet. On your visit to the kennel, note if it is clean and if they follow a daily cleanup schedule. Look for sturdy, high fencing, and dividers between the runs. Make sure the gates are secured with locks.

Check to see if the exercise areas provide protection from wind, rain, snow and direct sunlight. If there is a large fenced enclosure for dogs to exercise, make sure it is also well fenced and gates are kept securely locked. Advise the operators if your dog should be limited in his or her exercise due to a heart condition or other ailment. Also, let them know if your pet is a digger or a climber and could get under or over the fences.

Check out the inside kennels. They should be free of sharp objects or harmful chemicals that your pet might swallow. There should be no dirt, fecal matter, or parasite infestation (fleas, flies or ticks). Solid dividers should be between the sleeping areas so your pet can relax and sleep without being disturbed by other pets. Check to see if the sleeping area is clean and dry, and roomy enough for your pet to stand up comfortably, turn around easily, and stretch out. Find out about bedding for the pets. Some kennels provide resting platforms or bedding, others request that you bring bedding from home. Note if the kennels are temperature controlled so your pet is comfortable in summer and winter.

Check to see if each kennel has individual water bowls filled with clean drinking water. Many kennels supply their own food for the pets, however, many allow you to bring the food your pet is used to eating. Ask if there are extra charges for feeding arrangements. My Newfoundland has three meals a day, plus a snack. Fortunately, the kennel where we board him has no problem with this arrangement.

If your pet is on medication, some kennels will charge extra for giving your pet meds. Some kennels will refuse to give diabetes shots, so be sure to check. Some kennels have their own veterinarian on the premises, but other kennels would prefer to use the veterinarian that is accustomed to looking after your pet. Either way, you are responsible for any veterinary care your pet is given while in the care of the boarding facility.

Most kennels require your pet to have up-to-date vaccinations. Some kennels will accept a pet if he or she has had titer tests done, which determine if your dog has sufficient immunity to the various diseases that he might pick up from or transmit to other animals when boarding.

One thing that really bothers me about some kennels is the fact that the operators leave the kennel at 7 p.m. in the evening and are not back until 7 a.m. the next morning. What would happen if a dog bloated or had a seizure, or if a fire broke out? Who would be there to help the animals? I would never, under any circumstances, leave a dog or a cat at a kennel where someone was not on the premises twenty-four hours a day.

I have been fortunate to find a great kennel where we board Kodi. It is a small operation, owned by a husband and wife team, who devote time to each pet in their care. Kodi goes for a "country walk" daily. The runs are divided into sections so there is less stress for the pet. Each section has a television and music, and their "Rainy Day Lounge" is complete with TV, VCR, toys, and a futon, which is great for the dogs who are there for the first time or for older dogs so they can relax and feel comfortable. The owners bake homemade dog cookies for daytime snacks. During holidays or special occasions, they prepare home-cooked meals for the pets. I am fortunate to have found such a high-caliber kennel in my hometown.

When you pick up your pet from the kennel, try arrive during business hours when personnel are working in the kennel. Your pet will be excited to go home, so try to keep things as calm as possible. Wait a few hours before feeding your dog because dogs tend to gulp food and water when they are excited, which could cause problems.

Boarding cats is a little different than boarding dogs. They do not require the exercise space that a dog needs, but are happy to be housed in roomy enclosures. Some kennels provide play areas for cats that enjoy additional space. Each enclosure should contain a clean litter box and a water bowl.

Remember: If you visit the kennel beforehand and ask all the pertinent questions, your pet will have a wonderful vacation while you are enjoying yours.

Declawing Cats

Please, do not declaw your cat(s). Most of the world does not declaw cats, and it is illegal or banned in many countries, including England, Wales, Scotland, Italy, France, Germany, Austria, Switzerland, Sweden, The Netherlands, Northern Ireland, Denmark, Finland, Slovenia, Portugal, Belgium, Spain, Brazil, Australia, and New Zealand.

Many veterinarians in the United States and Canada refuse to declaw cats because they understand how devastating this can be for felines. In an information sheet on declawing, Matthew Ehrenberg, D.V.M., describes declawing as "an amputation of the toe at the last joint. This removes the claw and the bone from which it originates. On a human hand this would be an amputation at the knuckle just below the nail."[2]

Recovery from this procedure is painful and some of the surgical complications may include "inadvertent removal of part of a digital pad, incomplete removal of the nail bed and partial re-growth of the nail, infection, rare anesthetic complications." Cats can have disfigurement of the feet, lameness, psychological trauma, and the inability to defend against other animals.

Over the years, I have heard about many cats who have developed severe infections in their paws after declawing. Shelagh MacDonald from the Canadian Federation of Humane Societies (CFHS), writes, "Many veterinarians do not condone declawing as it can be a painful procedure that can cause ongoing discomfort and it robs the cat of a natural defense.

It should only be considered if all other options have been exhausted and it is the only alternative to euthanasia."[3]

Gary Loewenthal writes in the *Whole Cat Journal*, "Some veterinarians are now promoting laser declawing as a 'guilt-free' procedure. While laser declawing can reduce bleeding and perhaps diminish, to some extent, the agonizing pain, the procedure is no different, only the means of amputation."[4]

Scratching is an ingrained instinct in cats. In an article on why cats scratch, Glenda Moore writes, "While some people think a cat scratches to sharpen its claws, that is probably inaccurate. There are typically two reasons for scratching: the cat is marking its territory (cats have sweat glands between their paw pads, and scratching leaves their scent on the clawed object); or, the cat is 'filing down' its nails and removing the outer layer."[5]

Over the years I have shared my home with approximately twenty cats, and I have never had one declawed. They have scratching posts and large logs, which they love to scratch, but seldom have they ever used the furniture. A growing number of pet owners and veterinarians, as well as lawmakers in cities, states, and countries are speaking out against declawing of cats (and devocalization of dogs). They are condemning it as an unnecessary and inhumane procedure. We need to continue educating the general public on declawing as inhumane treatment.

—

There is a wonderful saying by Mohandas Gandhi, the great East Indian leader and teacher of nonviolence. I see this quote every so often on various pet sites. Gandhi said, "The greatness of a nation and its moral progress can be judged by the way its animals are treated."

Slowly, humanity is learning that our fellow animals are not "things" to use and abuse as we like, but rather co-inhabitants of earth. My hope is that we will treat our animal companions with greater care and respect, and in turn, we will extend our moral progress as human beings!

In memory of Louise, 1994~ 2005,
the publisher's beloved dog.
Louise loved the snow and
howling with distant coyotes.

PHOTO: MAUREEN MICHELSON

Resources

Suggested Reading Material

Anderson, N. Peiper H., DVM, *Are You Poisoning Your Pet?* East Canaan, Connecticut: Safe Goods Publishing, 1995.

Anderson, N., Peiper, H., DVM, *Super-Nutrition for Dogs n' Cats,* East Canaan, Connecticut: Safe Good Publisher, 2000.

Brown, Andi, *The Whole Pet Diet: Eight Weeks to Great Health for Dogs and Cats,* Berkley, California: Celestial Arts, 2006.

Congalton, D., Alexander, C., *When Your Pet Outlives You: Protecting Animal Companions After You Die,* Troutdale, Oregon: NewSage Press, 2002.

Downing, R., DVM, *Pets Living with Cancer,* Lakewood, Colorado: American Animal Hospital Association Press, 2000.

Eisnitz, G.A., *Slaughterhouse,* Amherst, New York: Prometheus Books, 1997.

Fox, M.W., DVM, *Eating with Conscience: The Bioethics of Food,* Troutdale, Oregon: NewSage Press, 1997.

Fox, M.W., DVM, *The Healing Touch For Dogs,* New York: Newmarket Press, 2004.

Fox, M.W., DVM, *The Healing Touch For Cats,* New York: Newmarket Press, 2004.

Goldstein, M., DVM, *The Nature of Animal Healing,* New York, New York: Alfred A. Knopf, 1999.

Houston, L., *Nobody's Best Friend,* Chester, New Jersey: MCE Press, 1998.

Martin, A. N., *Protect Your Pet: More Shocking Facts*, Troutdale, Oregon: NewSage Press, 2001.

Merwick, K., *People Food for Dogs,* Seattle, Washington: Elfin Cove Press, 1997.

Messonnier, S., DVM, *The Natural Vet's Guide to Prevent and Treating Cancer in Dogs,* Novato, California, New World Library, 2006.

Messonnier, S., DVM, *The Allergy Solution for Dogs: Natural and Conventional Therapies to Ease Discomfort and Enhance Your Dog's Quality of Life,* Roseville, California: Prima Publishing, 2000.

Messonnier, S., DVM, *Natural Health Bible for Dogs & Cats: Your A-Z Guide to Over 200 Conditions, Herbs, Vitamins, and Supplements,* Roseville, California: Prima Publishing, 2001.

Plechner, A., DVM, with Zucker, M., *Pets At Risk: From Allergies to Cancer, Remedies for an Unsuspected Epidemic,* Troutdale, Oregon: NewSage Press, 2003.

Schlosser, E., *Fast Food Nation: The Dark Side of the American Meal,* New York, New York: Houghton Mifflin, 2001.

Straw, D., *Why Is Cancer Killing Our Pets?* Rochester, Vermont: Healing Arts Press, 2000.

Straw, D., *The Healthy Pet Manual,* Rochester, Vermont: Healing Arts Press, 2005.

Strombeck, D.R., DVM, *Home Prepared Dog and Cat Diets,* Ames, Iowa: Iowa State University Press, 1999.

Zucker, M., *Natural Remedies for Cats,* New York, New York: Three Rivers Press, 1999.

Zucker, M. *Natural Remedies for Dogs,* New York, New York: Three Rivers Press, 1999.

Endnotes

Chapter One: *The Truth About Commercial Pet Foods*

1. Lee, Don, "China's additives on menu in U.S.," *Los Angeles Times*, May 18, 2007.

2. Berry, Kate, "Export ban leads to pileup of dead beasts at rendering plant facilities,"
Los Angeles Business Journal, March 22, 2004.

3. Grillo, Leo, "Food Poisoning: You Are Eating California's Dead Pets," Information Sheet, October 2, 2007.

4. Farah, Joseph, "Seafood Imports from China Raised in Untreated Sewage," *World News Daily,* June 4, 2007.

Chapter Two: *Unraveling the Mystery Ingredients*

1. Cooke, David C., "Euthanasia of the Companion Animal," Animal Disposal: Fact or Fiction," American Veterinarians Medical Association, Panel on Euthanasia, 1988, p. 227.

2. Personal correspondence with AAFCO, the Department of Agriculture, State of Delaware, September 23, 1994.

Chapter Three: *Questionable Vitamins, Minerals and Additives*

1. *CBC News*, Canada, "50M Lawsuit Filed Against Pet Food Company, " March 20, 2007.

2. The Dog Food Project, "Menadione (Vitamin K3)," Website, www.dogfoodproject.com/index.php?page=menadione

3. Griffith, H. Winter, *Complete Guide to Vitamins, Minerals and Other Supplements,* Tucson, Arizona: Fisher Books, 1988, p. 49.

4. Extoxnet Extension Toxicology Network, "Breakdown of Chemicals in Vegetation," Cornell University, Michigan State University, Oregon State University and University of California at Davis, Paper, May 1994.

5. Personal correspondence from Belfield,Wendell, DVM, to Sharon Benz, Center for Veterinary Medicine, letter, March 25, 2002.

6. The Animal Protection Institute, Investigative Report, May 2007.

7. Wirick, Steven J., "News and Announcements," Solid Gold Health Products for Pets, Inc., 2007.

CHAPTER FOUR: *Animal Carcasses as a Protein Source*

1. National Renderers Association, "Essential Rendering, All About the Animal By-Product Industry," Kirby Lithograph Company, Inc., Arlington, Virginia, 2006.

2. Personal correspondence with John Mays, National Animal Control Association, October 24, 2007.

3. Environmental Protection Act, Section 9.5.3, "Meat Rendering Plants," www.epa.gov/ttn/chief/ap42/ch09/final/c9s05-3.pdf.

4. Blakeslee, Sandra, "Disease Fear Prompts New Look at Rendering," *The New York Times,* March 11, 1997.

5. Personal correspondence with Alan Schulman, DVM, Los Angeles, California, July 24, 2000.

6. National Renderers Association, "Disposal (Rendering) of Deceased Animals from Los Angeles Country Animal Shelters." Fact Sheet, April 8, 2004.

7. Mortensen, Camilla, "The Road to No-Kill," *Eugene Weekly*, April 26, 2007.

8. Personal correspondence with John Mukhar, Senior Engineer for Environmental Enforcement, San Jose, October 31, 2007.

9. Food and Drug Administration, Center for Veterinary Medicine, "Food and Drug Administration/Center for Veterinary Medicine Report on the risk from pentobarbital in dog food," March 28, 2002. www.fda/gov/cvm/efoi/efoi/html

10. Myers, Michael J., PhD; Farrell, Dorothy, BS; Heller, David N., BS; Yancy, Haile, PhD, "Development of a polymerase chain reaction-based method to identify species-specific components in dog food," *American Journal of Veterinary Research*, Vol. 65, No. 1, January 2004.

11. Dorothy Farrell, Laboratory notes, June 28, 2001.

12. Personal correspondence with Joe Donnenhoffer, Roch Diagnostics, May 7, 2007.

13. Personal correspondence with Gene Weddington, PhD, May 24, 2001.

14. Faletra, Peter, PhD, "DNA and Heat," Office of Science, Department of Energy, University of Chicago, Molecular Biology, 2000. http://newton.dep.anl.gov/askasci/-mole00/mole00136.htm

15. Carlson, John, MD/PhD (parasitology), Tulane University, July, 23, 1999. www.madsci.org/posts/archives/jul99/932995255.Mb.r.html

16. Personal correspondence with Albert Harper, PhD, Director of The Henry C. Lee Institute of Forensic Science, University of New Haven, July 17, 2002.

17. Personal correspondence with Government of Quebec, Department of Food, Fisheries, and Agriculture, August 14, 1992.

18. Freeze, Colin, "Animal Feed to Exclude Cat, Dogs," *Globe and Mail,* June 4, 2001.

19. Lee-Shanok, Philip, "Is Your Animal a Cannibal?" *Toronto Sun,* June 7, 2001.

20. Personal correspondence with Mario Couture, Rendering Procurement Office, November 9, 2007.

21. Personal correspondence with Isabelle Trudeau, Ministry of Agriculture, Quebec, June 6, 2001.

22. Rothsay, "Backgrounder on Ministry of Environment Issues and Rothsay Dundas," Community News, Website, November 1, 2005. www.rothsay.ca/dundas.html#about_rothsay

23. Ibid.

CHAPTER FIVE: *Sodium Pentobarbital in Pet Food*

1. Personal correspondence with Lori L. Miser, DVM, Illinois Department of Agriculture, Bureau of Animal Health, March 11, 2002.

2. "2000 Report of the American Veterinary Medical Association Panel on Euthanasia," *Journal of the American Veterinary Medical Association,* Vol. 218, No. 5, March 1, 2001, p. 685.

3. Ibid.

4. O'Connor, John J., DVM, MPH; Stowe, Clarence M.,VMD, PhD; Robinson, Robert R., BVSc, MPH, PhD, "Fate of Sodium Pentobarbital in Rendered Material," *American Journal of Veterinary Research,* Vol. 46, No. 8, August 1995, pp. 1721-1723.

5. United States Animal Health Association, "Report of the USAHA Committee on Feed Safety," 1998 Committee Report, October 7, 1998.

6. Personal correspondence with Wanda Russ, Policy Analyst, FDA, Executive Secretariat, February 8, 2001.

7. Food and Drug Administration, Center for Veterinary Medicine, "Food and Drug Administration/Center for Veterinary Medicine, Report on the risk from pentobarbital in dog food," March 28, 2002. www.fda/gov/cvm/efoi/efoi/html

8. Ibid.

9. Ibid.

10. Kawakejm, Joseph; Howard, Karyn; Farrell, Dorothy; Derr, Janice; Cope, Carol; Jackon, Jean; Myers, Michael, "Effect of oral administration of low doses of pentobarbital on the induction of cytochrome P450 isoforms and cytochrome P450-mediated reactions in immature beagles," *American Journal of Veterinary Research,* Vol. 64, pp. 1167-1175, 2003.

11. Ibid.

12. Animal Ark, "Study Finds Euthanasia Agent in Pet Foods," *Report*, March 30, 2002.

13. Personal correspondence with Stephen Sundlof, DVM, Center for Veterinary Medicine, May 18, 2005.

14. Miser, Lori L., opt. cit.

15. California Department of Food and Agriculture, Animal Health and Food Safety Services, Animal Care Program, "The Emergency Euthanasia of Horses," Information Sheet, November 1999.

16. National Euthanasia Registry, www.usner.org/press.htm

17. Ibid.

Chapter Six: *Pet Food Regulations*

1. Benz, Sharon, PhD, "FDA's Regulation of Pet Food," Information for Consumers, Fact Sheet, 2001.

2. Personal correspondence with Rodney Noel, DVM, Indiana Associate State Chemist, April 16, 2007.

3. Personal correspondence with Robert Hougaard, Program Manager, Utah Department of Agriculture and Food, April 18, 2007.

4. Personal correspondence with David Shang, Department of Agriculture, New Jersey, April 19, 2005.

5. Personal correspondence with Arty Schronce, Georgia Department of Agriculture, April 18, 2007.

6. Department of Agriculture, "Association of American Feed Control Officials Feed Check Sample Program," State of Colorado, Information Sheet, 2001.

7. Personal correspondence with Nancy Cook, VP of Technical and Regulatory Affairs, Pet Food Institute, April 28, 2000.

8. Pet Food Institute, "A Consumers Guide to Pet Foods," Report, September 2002.

9. Personal correspondence with Denise Spencer, DVM, Senior Staff Veterinarian, United States Department of Agriculture, National Center for Import and Export, January 8, 2002.

10. Personal correspondence with Vic Powell, USDA, April 17, 2007.

11. Government of Canada, Canadian Food Inspection Agency, "Animal Health and Production Division: Import Procedures," Regulations, April 6, 2001.

12. European Economic Council, "Guidelines for pet food exports to Europe," Council Directive 90/667/Eurasian Economic Community (EEC), April 1997.

13. The Pet Food Manufacturer's Association, U.K., 2001. www.pfma.com/about.htm

14. Personal correspondence with Alison Walker, spokesperson for the Pet Food Manufacturers Association, U.K., March 19, 2002.

15. The Japanese Market News, "Pet Food," 2001. www.wtcjapan.ne.jp/jmn/petfood.html

CHAPTER SEVEN: *Pet Food Manufacturers*

1. Euromonitor International, "Pet Foods and Accessories in the USA," Report, October 2005.

2. Institute of Food Science and Engineering, "Kal Kan Pet Care," Texas A&M University, Paper, 2001.

3. Cowdy, Hannah, "Royal Canin pet food buy makes Mars Europe top dog," Reuters, July 10, 2001.

4. KMOV-TV, St. Louis Missouri, "FTC approves Nestlé's $10.3 billion purchase of Ralston Purina," Report, December 11, 2001.

5. Federal Trade Commission, "Analysis of Proposed Consent Order to Aid Public Comment," Paper, December 11, 2001.

6. Gibbs, Gordon, "More Court Dates on the Menu in the Wake of Menu Foods Recall," *Lawyers and Settlements,* July 8, 2007.

7. Weise, Elizabeth, "Court: Menu Foods harassed pet owners," *USA Today*, May 26, 2007.

8. College of Veterinary Medicine and Biomedical Sciences, Executive Council Minutes, June 8, 2000.

9. Student Chapter of the American Veterinary Medical Association, "Hill's Food Orders," University of Colorado, Information Sheet, February 2007.

10. Nestlé Purina Veterinary College Program, Information Sheet, 2007.

11. Word Press, "Claudia Kirk, Shank for the pet food industry," website, www.lethaldose.wordpress.com/2007/04/06/claudia-kirk-dvm-skank-for-the-pet-food-industry.

12. *Journal of the American Veterinary Medical Association*, "Hill's Provides Impressive Funding for Future Conventions," Newsletter, December 1, 2003.

13. The Humane Society of the United States, "Hill's Science Diet Signed as Major Sponsor of HSUS Programs," *Companion Animal Update*, Newsletter, February 2002.

14. Ibid.

15. American Kennel Club, Canine Health Foundation, "AKC Canine Health Foundation Founders Club," Information Sheet, 2003.

CHAPTER EIGHT: *Pet Food Recalls*

1. Johnson, Mark, "Lab Gets New Attention in Pet Food Case," Associated Press, April 1, 2007.

2. Staats, Jim, "Marin case confirms new tainted pet food," *Marin Independent Journal*, April 9, 2007.

3. Testimony by Stephen F. Sundlof, DVM, PhD, Pet Food Hearing Transcripts, April 12, 2007.

4. Testimony by Duane Ekedahl, Pet Food Hearing Transcript, April 12, 2007.

5. Ibid.

6. Ibid.

7. Patterson, Ashleigh, *CTV News*, "Scientists track chemical reactions in pet food," Report, April 27, 2007.

8. Barboza, David, "China finds two companies guilty in tainted pet food export," *International Herald Tribune*, May 8, 2007.

9. Phillips, Tim, "Menu CEO talks recalls," *Pet Food Industry Magazine*, September 18, 2007.

10. Lee, Don and Goldman, Abigail, "Factory linked to tainted food found closed," *Los Angeles Times*, May 11, 2007.

11. Schmit, Julie, "Pet food probe: Who was watching suppliers?" *USA Today*, May 11, 2007.

12. Food and Drug Administration, "Pet Food Recall/Contaminated Feed, Update Report," August 1, 2007.

13. "U.S. Food Imports Rarely Inspected," Associated Press, April 16, 2007.

14. Food and Drug Administration, Department of Health and Human Services, "Inspectional Observations," Diamond Pet Food Processors of South Carolina, Gaston, South Carolina. December 21, 2005 to January 19, 2006.

15. Lang, Susan, "Dogs keep dying," Cornell University, *Chronicle Online*, Updated, January 17, 2006.

16. *FDA News*, "FDA Warns Consumers Not to Use Wild Kitty Cat Food Due to Salmonella Contamination," February 13, 2007.

17. Barboza, David, and Barrionuevo, Alexei, "Filler In Animal Feed Is Open Secret In China," *New York Times*, April 30, 2007.

Chapter Nine: *Animal Experimentation and Pet Food Companies*

1. The Massachusetts Society for the Prevention of Cruelty to Animals, "Product Safety Testing," 2006. www.mspca.org/site/PageServer?pagename=advo_Lab_Animals_Product_SafeTest

2. Stoick, Kristie, "Ohio State University: A Year of Cruelty," *Physicians Committee for Responsible Medicine Magazine*, Winter, 2007, Volume XVI, Number 1.

3. Stop Animal Tests, "Whistleblower Exposes Cruel Cat Experiments at UC Denver and Health Science Center," Report, February 2007.

4. O'Donnell, Noreen, "New York Medical College May Discontinue Dog Labs," *New York's Lower Hudson Valley*, November 14, 2007. www.lohud.com/apps/pbcs.dll/article?AID=/20071114/NEWS01/711140357/1265/columnist25.

5. Johnston, Lucy, Health Editor, "Iams-Pet Food Cruelty Exposed," *Sunday Express,* May 27, 2001.

6. Uncaged Campaigns, "Iams—The Suffering Behind the Science," June 1, 2001. www.uncaged.co.uk/iams.htm.

7. Animal People Online, "Pet Food and Procter and Gamble," June 2001. http://207.36.38.241/01/6/petfoodAP0601.html.

8. PETA, "The Rotten Truth Behind Iams' 'Dental Defense's Diet." www.iamscruelty.com/iams-feat-dental.asp.

9. Keep On Fighting, "Iams Kills 32 Great Dane Puppies," May 14, 2004. www.keeponfighting.net/article.php?story=20040514061955564

10. Care2, "Iams Cruelty," April 9, 2005. www.care2.com/c2c/groups/disc.html?gpp=3600&pst=71216&archival=1

11. The Group for the Education of Animal-Related Issues (GEARI), "Sinclair Research Center Recent Animal Testing Facility to be Found Guilty of Committing Nearly 40 Violations of the Federal Animal Welfare Act," March 27, 2007. http://geari.blogspot.com/2007/03/sinclair-research-center-recent-animal.html.

12. Ibid.

13. Stop Cruelty, "Procter & Gamble Animal Testing," www.iamsagainstcruelty.com/iac/jsp/factsHistory/P&GAnimalTesting.jsp.

14. Personal correspondence with Shalin Gala, Senior Researcher, PETA, February 26, 2008.

15. Carter-Long, Lawrence, "Stop Torturing Animals for Pet Food Research," Animal Protection Institute, Press release, August 6, 2001.

16. Alternative Veterinary Medicine Center, "Alternative Medicine for Animals," www.alternativevet.org

17. *Journal of Animal Physiology & Animal Nutrition*, vol. 87, 2003, pp. 315-323.

18. British Union for the Abolition of Vivisection, "In The Can-Pet Food Tests Expose," Press release, June 2000.

19. Ibid.

20. PETA, " Menu Foods Animal Tests: A PETA Investigation," 2002-2003. www.peta.org/feat/iams/menu-video.html.

21. Benjamin, David, Letter to Len Sauers, Procter & Gamble Company, March 21, 2007.

22. Born Free, "What's Really In Pet Food," May 2007. www.api4animals.org/facts.php?p=359&more=1

CHAPTER TEN: *Natural Pet Food Companies*

1. Strombeck, Donald R., DVM, PhD, *Home Prepared Dog and Cat Diets*, Iowa State University Press, Ames, Iowa, 1999, p 8.

2. Plechner, Alfred J., DVM, with Zucker, Martin, *Pets At Risk: From Allergies to Cancer, Remedies for an Unsuspected Epidemic*," NewSage Press, Troutdale, Oregon, 2003, p 6.

3. Editorial, "The Biggest Recall Ever," *The New York Times*, February 21, 2008.

4. Personal correspondence with Alex Beinart, Halo, Purely for Pets, March 18, 2008.

5. Mulligan Stew™ Pet Food, "Unleashing the Next Revolution in Pet Nutrition," www.mulliganstewpetfood.com.

6. Personal correspondence with Peter Atkins, Natura, August 8, 2007.

7. Personal correspondence with L. Phillips Brown, DVM, Corporate Veterinarian, Newman's Own® Organics, July 1, 2007.

8. Personal correspondence with Peter Muhlenfeld, Orijen Pet Foods, July 16, 2007.

9. Personal correspondence with Michele Dixon, Petcurean, July 9, 2007. Petcurean website, www.petcurean.com.

10. Personal correspondence with Leasa Greer, Solid Gold Health Products for Pets, July 27, 2007.

11. Personal correspondence with Joseph Carey, Timberwolf Organics, June 29, 2007.

12. Johnson, Tim, "China corners vitamin market," *The Seattle Times,* June 3, 2007.

13. Schmit, Julie; Weise, Elizabeth, "Chinese imports nixed by key firm," *USA Today,* June 5, 2007.

14. Goldstein, David, "Tainted Wheat Gluten Sold as Human Grade," *Huffington Post*, April 1, 2007.

CHAPTER ELEVEN: *Cooking for Cats*

1. Pion, P.D.; Kittleson, M.D.; Rogers, Q.R.; Morris, J.G., "Myocardial failure in cats associated with low plasma taurine; a reversible cardiomyopathy," *Science*, Vol. 237, Issue 4816, pp. 764-768.

2. Foster, Rory, DVM; Smith, Marty, DVM, "Protein Requirements for Good Nutrition," www.peteducation.com/article.cfm?cls=1&articleid=701, 2007.

3. Vegetarian Society of the United Kingdom, "Cats—a vegetarian diet?" Information paper, www.vegsoc.org/info/catfood.html.

4. Foster, Rory, DVM; Smith, Marty, DVM, "Carbohydrates as Energy Sources in Cat Foods," Paper, 2007.

5. Ibid.

6. Ibid.

7. Plechner, Alfred, DVM, with Zucker, Martin, "*Pets At Risk: From Allergies to Cancer, Remedies for an Unsuspected Epidemic*," NewSage Press, Troutdale, Oregon, 2003, p. 43.

8. Mangels, Reed, PhD, RD, "Guide to Grains," *Vegetarian Journal*, Sept/Oct 1999. www.vrg.org/journal/vj99sep/999grains.htm.

9. Roehl, Evelyn, "Quinoa from the Andes," Whole Food Facts, *Healing Arts Press*, Rochester, Vermont, 1996.

10. Putnam, D.H.; Oplinger, E.S.; Doll, J.D.; and Schulte, E.M., *Alternative Field Crops Manual*, "Amaranth." www.hort.purdue.edu/newcrop/afcm/amaranth.html

11. Dunn, T.J., DVM, "Fatty Acids, You and Your Pet," The Pet Center.com. www.thepetcenter.com/gen/fa.html.

12. The Vegetarian Society of the United Kingdom, "Cats—A Vegetarian Diet?" Information Sheet, 2007.

13. Provet Healthcare Information, "Vitamin A." www.provet.co.uk/petfacts/healthtips/vitamina.htm.

14. Plechner, Alfred, DVM, opt. cit.

15. Strieker, M.J.; Morris, J.G.; Feldman, B.F.; Rogers, Q.R., "Vitamin K deficiency in cats fed commercial fish-based diets," Paper, July 1996, Department of Molecular Biology, School of Veterinary Medicine, University of California.

16. Houpt, K.A.; Essick, L.A.; Shaw, E.B.; Alo, D.K.; Gilmartin, J.E.; Gutenmann, W.H.; Littman, C.B.; Lisk, D.J., "A tuna fish diet influences cat behavior," Paper, 1988, Department of Physiology, Cornell University, New York State College of Veterinary Medicine.

17. Nowell, Kristine; Jackson, Peter, "Wild Cats, Status Survey and Conservation Action Plan IUCN/SSC Cat Specialist Group," p. 32, 1996.

18. Kass, P.H.; Peterson, M.E.; Levy, J.; James, K.; Becker, D.V.; Cowgill, L.D., "Evaluation of environmental, nutritional, and host factors in cats with hyperthyroidism," July-August 1999, Department of Population and Reproduction, School of Veterinary Medicine, University of California.

19. Ibid.

20. Edinboro, C.H.; Scott-Moncrieff, J.C.; Janovitz, E.; Thacker, H.L.; Glickman, L.T., "Epidemiologic study of relationships between consumption of commercial canned food and risk of hyperthyroidism in cats," *Journal of the American Veterinary Medical Association*, May 2004, vol. 224, pp. 879-86.

CHAPTER TWELVE: *Recipes for Cats*

1. Healthy Recipes for Pets, "Cat Food Recipes, www.healthyrecipesforpets.com/cat_food_recipes.html.

2. Ibid.

3. Plechner, Alfred, DVM, with Martin Zucker, *Pets at Risk: From Allergies to Cancer, Remedies for an Unsuspected Epidemic*, NewSage Press, Troutdale, Oregon, 2003, p. 43.

4. Ibid., p.108-109.

5. Healthy Recipes for Pets, op.cit.

6. Cat Treat Recipes Using Meat, Chicken and Turkey. www.nocans.com/cat-meat-treats.html.

CHAPTER THIRTEEN: *Cooking For Dogs*

1. Goldstein, Martin, DVM, "*The Nature of Animal Healing*, New York, New York, Ballantine Books, 1999, p. 127.

2. "Quinoa, Soul Food of the Andes," www.vegparadise.com/highestperch36.html.

3. Brown, Andi, "*The Whole Pet Diet*," Celestial Arts, Berkeley, California, 2006, p. 67.

4. Messonnier, Shawn, "Using Whole Food Supplements to Treat a Common Skin Disorder," *Pet Care*. www.petcarenaturally.com/articles/using-whole-food-supplements.php

5. Plechner, Alfred J., D.V.M., with Martin Zucker, *"Pets At Risk: From Allergies to Cancer, Remedies for an Unsuspected Epidemic,"* NewSage Press, Troutdale, Oregon, 2003.

6. Zucker, Martin, *"Natural Remedies for Dogs,"* New York, New York, Three Rivers Press, 1999, p 44.

7. Belfield, Wendell, DVM; Zucker, Martin, *How to Have a Healthier Dog,* New York, New York, Doubleday and Company, 1981, p 89.

8. Contreras, Sabine, "Canine Care and Nutrition," The Dog Food Project. www.dogfoodproject.com/index.php?page=myths

9. Koelkebeck, Ken W., DVM, "What is Egg Shell Quality and How to Preserve It," Department of Animal Sciences, University of Illinois, 2007. http://ag.ansc.purdue.edu/poultry/multistate/koelkebeck1.htm

10. Fascetti, A.J.; Rogers, Q.R.; Backus, R.C.; Cohen, G.; Pion, P.D.; Good, K.L., "Taurine deficiency in Newfoundlands fed commercially available complete and balanced diets," *Journal of the America Veterinary Medical Association,* Vol. 223, No. 8, pp. 1130-1136, 2003.

11. The Vegetarian Society, "Dogs, a Vegetarian Diet," Information Sheet. www.vegsoc.org/info/dogfood1.html.

12. Pitcairn, Richard, DVM, "Using Calcium In Home Prepared Diets." www.drpitcairn.com/books/pitcairn_book.html

13. Ibid.

CHAPTER FOURTEEN: *Recipes For Dogs*

1. American Society for the Prevention of Cruelty to Animals, Animal Poison Control Center, Paper, 2007.

2. Doggie Connection, www.doggieconnection.com/recipe.

3. Sweetie's Yorkie Web World. www.geocities.com/Heartland/Pointe/9350/recipes.html.

4. Plechner, Alfred J., DVM with Zucker, Martin, *Pets at Risk: From Allergies to Cancer, Remedies for an Unsuspected Epidemic,* NewSage Press, Troutdale, Oregon, 2003, p. 43.

5. Healthy Recipes for Dogs. www.healthyrecipesforpets.com/dog_food_recipes.html.

6. Good Dog Express. www.gooddogexpress.com/recipes.htm.

7. Pet Meds On Line, Homemade Vegetarian Dog Treats. www.petmedsonline.org/homemade-vegetarian-dog-treats.html

8. BarkBarkImHungry.com, www.barkbarkimhungry.com.

9. Pet Meds On Line, op.cit.

Chapter Fifteen: *Bloat: A Canine Killer*

1. Feinman, Jeff, VMD, CVH, "Bloat," from Dr. Feinman's Library, www.homevet.com/brochure.html#vet, 1996.

2. Bell, Jerold S., DVM, "Healthy Dog," Article, Tufts University School of Veterinary Medicine, Canine and Feline Breeding and Genetics Conference, April 2003.

3. Raghaven, M, et al, "Diet-related risk factors for gastric dilation-volvulus in dogs of high-risk breeds," *Journal of the American Animal Health Association*, 40:192-2003, 2004.

4. Ibid., Bell, Jerold, DVM.

5. "Bloat: The Mother of All Emergencies." www.marvistavet.com/html/body_bloat.html

6. Glickman, Lawrence, VMD, Dr.PH; Glickman, Nita W., MS, MPH; Schellenberg, Diana B., MS; Raghaven, Malathi, DVM, MS; Lee, Tana, BA, "Canine Gastric Dilatation-Volvulus (Bloat)," *Journal of the American Veterinary Medical Association*, 2000; 216 (1) pp. 40-45.

7. Ibid.

8. Bell, Jerold, DVM., opt. cit.

9. Glickman, Lawrence, T., VMD, opt. cit.

Chapter Sixteen: *Other Pet Concerns*

1. Plechner, Alfred J., D.V.M., with Martin Zucker, *Pets At Risk: From Allergies to Cancer, Remedies for an Unsuspected Epidemic*, NewSage Press, Troutdale, Oregon, 2003, p. 9.

2. Ehrenbery, Matthew, "The Ethics of Declawing," Information Sheet, 1999.

3. Canadian Federation of Humane Societies, "Happy Indoor Cats," Fact sheet, July 1998.

4. Loewenthal, Gary, "Why Cats Need Claws," *Whole Cat Journal*, September 2002.

5. Moore, Glenda, "Why Does A Cat Do That?" www.xmission.com/~emailbox/whycat.htm.

PHOTO: MARY CHAMBERS

*A*NN N. MARTIN is recognized as an international authority on the commercial pet food controversy. Since 1990, Martin has investigated and questioned exactly what goes into most commercial pet food as well as the multi-billion dollar, self-regulated pet food industry.

The first edition of *Food Pets Die For: Shocking Facts About Pet Food*, published in 1997, was the first book to expose the hazards of commercial pet food. In 2003, the second edition of *Food Pets Die For* was published, launching Martin's book as a grassroots bestseller. Her second book, *Protect Your Pet: More Shocking Facts*, was published by NewSage Press in 2001, providing readers with additional information on issues related to pet health and pet-related issues.

Sonoma State University's journalism awards for *Project Censored* honored Martin's investigative reporting on the commercial pet food industry, acknowledging this as "one of the most censored news stories of 1997." *Project Censored* focuses on important news events that are largely ignored by mainstream media. Martin has been on numerous television and radio shows internationally, and interviewed by major newspapers in the United States and Canada, particularly during the 2007 pet food recall. *Food Pets Die For* has been translated into Japanese.

Martin graduated with a B.A. in business from the University of Western Ontario, and worked in a tax office for several years. She lives with her family and animal companions in Ontario, Canada, where she continues to research and write about pet-related issues.

She can be reached by email at anmartin1@rogers.com or you can reach her through NewSage Press's website.

www.newsagepress.com

Protect Your Pet: More Shocking Facts

In her second book, *Protect Your Pet* (NewSage Press 2001), Ann Martin continues her thorough investigation of pet-related issues. She examines the popular raw meat diet; the latest information on the controversy surrounding yearly vaccinations; increased cancer in pets and over-vaccination; alternatives in vaccination protocols; and the latest on the controversy of using Rimadyl for arthritic dogs. The final chapter offers more healthy homemade recipes for cats and dogs.

Praise for Protect Your Pet

The pet food industry and its allies dictate thinking for pet owners and veterinarians on feeding pets. *Protect Your Pet* discusses important problems the industry refuses to address. It also documents truths on other issues that veterinarians choose to ignore. This book is an essential resource that all pet owners should read.

—DONALD R. STROMBECK, DVM, PhD
Professor Emeritus, UC Davis, School of Veterinary Medicine
Author, *Home Prepared Dog and Cat Diets*

This informative book offers excellent information that will help the pet owner to determine which diets are most beneficial. Good health can only be accomplished through good nutrition.

—WENDELL BELFIELD, DVM
Author, *How to Have a Healthier Dog*

In *Food Pets Die For,* which has sold more than 20,000 copies, Ann N. Martin censured the pet food industry with meticulous evidence of contaminants in commercial food that can cause degenerative diseases and even death…. Though it may provoke disgust and outrage, pet owners who want the best for their cats and dogs should read this book.

—*Publishers Weekly*

201

NewSage Press has published several titles related to animals. We hope these books will inspire humanity towards a more compassionate and respectful treatment of all living beings.

Protect Your Pet: More Shocking Facts
by Ann N. Martin

Pets at Risk: From Allergies to Cancer, Remedies for an Unsuspected Epidemic
by Alfred J. Plechner, D.V.M. *with* Martin Zucker

When Your Pet Outlives You: Protecting Animal Companions After You Die
by David Congalton & Charlotte Alexander
Award Winner, CWA Muse Medallion 2002

Blessing the Bridge:
What Animals Teach Us About Death, Dying, and Beyond
by Rita M. Reynolds

Three Cats, Two Dogs, One Journey Through Multiple Pet Loss
by David Congalton
Award Winner, Merial Human-Animal Bond, Best Book

Conversations with Animals: Cherished Messages and Memories
as Told by an Animal Communicator
by Lydia Hiby with Bonnie Weintraub

Polar Dream: The First Solo Expedition by a Woman and
Her Dog to the Magnetic North Pole
by Helen Thayer, Foreword by Sir Edmund Hillary

Whales: Touching the Mystery (book and DVD set)
by Doug Thompson

Horse Nation: True Stories About Horses and People
by Teresa Tsimmu Martino

 NEWSAGE PRESS, PO Box 607, Troutdale, OR 97060-0607
Phone Toll Free 877-695-2211
Email: info@newsagepress.com, or www.newsagepress.com
Distributed to bookstores by Perseus (Publishers Group West)